DESIGN OF STEEL AND RCC STRUCTURE

AUTHOR

Dr. Sparsh Johari
Assistant Professor
Department of Civil Engineering,
Indian Institute of Technology Guwahati, Assam

REVIEWER

Dr. Mahendra Kumar Pal
Assistant Professor
Department of Civil Engineering,
Indian Institute of Technology (BHU) Varanasi, Uttar Pradesh

KHANNA BOOK PUBLISHING CO. (P) Ltd.
4C/4344, Ansari Road, Darya Ganj,
New Delhi, India

All India Council for Technical Education
Nelson Mandela Marg, Vasant Kunj,
New Delhi, India

Dear Readers,

To prevent the piracy, this book is secured with HIGH SECURITY HOLOGRAM on the front title cover. In case you don't find the hologram on the front cover title, please write us to at contact@khannabooks.com or whatsapp us at +91-99109 09320 and avail special gift voucher for yourself.

Specimen of Hologram on front Cover title:

Moreover, there is a SPECIAL DISCOUNT COUPON for you with EVERY HOLOGRAM.

How to avail this SPECIAL DISCOUNT:

Step 1: Scratch the hologram

Step 2: Under the scratch area, your "coupon code" is available

Step 3: Logon to www.khannabooks.com

Step 4: Use your "coupon code" in the shopping cart and get your copy at a special discount

Step 5: Enjoy your reading!

ISBN: 978-93-5538-836-0

Book Code: DIP492EN

Design of Steel and RCC Structure

by Dr. Sparsh Johari

First Edition: 2026

Originally Published by:

All India Council for Technical Education, Ministry of Education, GOI

Exclusively Published & Distributed by:

Khanna Book Publishing Co. (P) Ltd.

4C/4344, Ansari Road, Daryaganj,
New Delhi (INDIA)

Visit us at: **www.khannabooks.com**

Write us at: **contact@khannabooks.com**

To view complete list of books,
Please scan the QR Code:

Printed in Bharat.

प्रो. टी. जी. सीताराम
अध्यक्ष
Prof. T. G. Sitharam
Chairman

सत्यमेव जयते

आज़ादी का अमृत महोत्सव

अखिल भारतीय तकनीकी शिक्षा परिषद्
(भारत सरकार का एक सांविधिक निकाय)
(शिक्षा मंत्रालय, भारत सरकार)
नेल्सन मंडेला मार्ग, वसंत कुंज, नई दिल्ली–110070
दूरभाष : 011–26131498
ई–मेल : chairman@aicte-india.org

ALL INDIA COUNCIL FOR TECHNICAL EDUCATION
(A STATUTORY BODY OF THE GOVT. OF INDIA)
(Ministry of Education, Govt. of India)
Nelson Mandela Marg, Vasant Kunj, New Delhi-110070
Phone : 011-26131498
E-mail : chairman@aicte-india.org

FOREWORD

Engineers are the backbone of any modern society. They are the ones responsible for the marvels as well as the improved quality of life across the world. Engineers have driven humanity towards greater heights in a more evolved and unprecedented manner.

The All India Council for Technical Education (AICTE), have spared no efforts towards the strengthening of the technical education in the country. AICTE is always committed towards promoting quality Technical Education to make India a modern developed nation emphasizing on the overall welfare of mankind.

An array of initiatives has been taken by AICTE in last decade which have been accelerated now by the National Education Policy (NEP) 2020. The implementation of NEP under the visionary leadership of Hon'ble Prime Minister of India envisages the provision for education in regional languages to all, thereby ensuring that every graduate becomes competent enough and is in a position to contribute towards the national growth and development through innovation & entrepreneurship.

One of the spheres where AICTE had been relentlessly working since past couple of years is providing high quality original technical contents at Under Graduate & Diploma level prepared and translated by eminent educators in various Indian languages to its aspirants. For students pursuing 2nd year of their Engineering education, AICTE has identified 87 books, which shall be translated into 12 Indian languages - Hindi, Tamil, Gujarati, Odia, Bengali, Kannada, Urdu, Punjabi, Telugu, Marathi, Assamese & Malayalam. In addition to the English medium, books in different Indian Languages are going to support the students to understand the concepts in their respective mother tongue.

On behalf of AICTE, I express sincere gratitude to all distinguished authors, reviewers and translators from the renowned institutions of high repute for their admirable contribution in a record span of time.

AICTE is confident that these outcomes based original contents shall help aspirants to master the subject with comprehension and greater ease.

(Prof. T. G. Sitharam)

ACKNOWLEDGMENT

I am deeply grateful to the authorities of AICTE, particularly Prof T G Sitharam, Chairman; Dr Abhay Jere, Vice-Chairman; Prof. Rajive Kumar, Member-Secretary, Dr. Sunil Luthra, Director and Reena Sharma, Hindi Officer Training and Learning Bureau, for allowing me to write this book. Their meticulous planning and unwavering support in publishing the book on 'Design of Steel and RCC Structures' has been instrumental. I also sincerely appreciate the book reviewer, Dr Mahendra Kumar Pal, Assistant Professor, Department of Civil Engineering, Indian Institute of Technology (BHU) Varanasi, for his invaluable inputs across all book units.

This book is a testament to the collective wisdom and shared vision of the Government of India, AICTE members, experts, and authors who have generously shared their insights to advance engineering education in our country. I extend my heartfelt acknowledgments to the numerous contributors in this field whose published books, review articles, papers, photographs, footnotes, references, advice, and other valuable information have enriched my work.

I wish to acknowledge the support and great love of my family: my wife, Mrs. Shikha Mittal; my mother, Mrs. Nidhi Johari; my father, Mr. Ashok Kumar Johari; my sister-in-law, Mrs. Shubham Srivastava; and my brother, Mr. Utkarsh Johri. I am also thankful to my kid, Mr Ridhaan Johari, nephew, Mr Ivaan Johri, and maternal uncle, Late (Col) N B Saxena. They kept me going, and this work would not have been possible without their love and support.

Dr. Sparsh Johari

CONTRIBUTORS

I want to thank the following students for their contribution in shaping this book:

Mr Ashwini Kumar (Research scholar, IIT Guwahati)

Mr Rohit Sahu (Research scholar, IIT Guwahati)

Mr Sudarshan Saikia (Research scholar, IIT Guwahati)

Mr Parmarth Saini (Master's student, IIT Guwahati)

Mr Rahul Kumar Gupta (Master's student, IIT Guwahati)

Mr Rushil Rupen Vashi (Master's student, IIT Guwahati)

Mr Suryadip Rajendra Patil (Master's student, IIT Guwahati)

Dr. Sparsh Johari

PREFACE

Structural design is a critical field in civil engineering, where the strength, stability, and durability of buildings and infrastructure projects are paramount. In this rapidly evolving industry, the ability to design safe and efficient structures is an essential skill for engineers at all levels. This book, Design of Steel and RCC Structures, provides a comprehensive guide for diploma students, helping them understand the core principles and practical applications involved in designing structural elements made of steel and reinforced cement concrete (RCC). These two materials are the backbone of modern construction, and knowledge of their design is fundamental to the education of aspiring engineers.

The design process is a blend of theoretical concepts and practical solutions. Structural engineers must have a strong grasp of the underlying principles of mechanics, material science, and strength of materials, as well as a clear understanding of how to apply these principles in real-world situations. Steel and RCC are two of the most widely used materials in construction, each with unique properties, advantages, and challenges. Integrating both materials in one book exposes readers to various structural design techniques, enhancing their problem-solving abilities.

This book is designed to cater to diploma students' needs, providing theoretical knowledge and practical skills in structural design. The content is presented in a manner that encourages active learning, with numerous examples, illustrations, and step-by-step explanations of the design processes. Each chapter covers essential topics, such as material properties, load calculations, and the application of design codes and standards. Students will be introduced to designing individual structural components, such as beams and columns, using steel and RCC materials.

The book's first part focuses on the design of steel structures, which are renowned for their strength, versatility, and ability to withstand heavy loads. The design of steel members, such as beams and columns, requires a deep understanding of axial loads, bending, shear, and torsion. In addition, issues like buckling and lateral-torsional buckling must be considered, especially in the design of compression members. The book explains the use of different steel sections and their applications, helping students make informed decisions when choosing materials and shapes for structural elements.

The book's second part delves into the design of RCC structures, which are commonly used for their durability, versatility, and ability to resist various loading conditions. Reinforced concrete members like beams and columns are designed to resist bending, shear, and axial forces, often in combination. The design of RCC structures requires understanding the behavior of concrete under stress and the role of reinforcement in controlling cracks and maintaining structural integrity. The book covers both limit state and working stress methods of design, adhering to the relevant design codes such as IS 456:2000 for concrete structures and IS 800-2007 for steel structures.

Design of Steel and RCC Structures is an essential resource for diploma students in civil engineering who seek to develop a solid foundation in structural design. This book aims to equip students with the necessary knowledge and skills to succeed academically and professionally by offering a well-rounded approach covering steel and concrete structures. Through clear explanations, practical examples, and an emphasis on design codes and standards, this book serves as a stepping stone toward mastering the art of structural design and contributing to the safe and efficient construction of the built environment.

I hope this book is valuable and inspires students to embark on a fulfilling structural engineering journey. Whether you're involved in building towering skyscrapers, intricate infrastructure projects, or sustainable residential developments, I trust that the insights gleaned from this book will empower you to tackle challenges, drive innovation, and contribute to the continued advancement of the construction industry.

Happy reading, and best wishes for your structural engineering endeavors!

Dr. Sparsh Johari

OUTCOME-BASED EDUCATION

New Education Policy, NEP-2020 based education comprises of outcome-based curriculum, outcome-based teaching-learning process and outcome-based assessment to achieve targeted learning outcomes. As per National Board of Accreditation, after completion of diploma program in engineering and technology the graduate will be able to:

PO-1: Basic and discipline specific knowledge: Apply knowledge of basic mathematics, science, and engineering fundamentals and engineering specialization to solve the engineering problems.

PO-2: Problem analysis: Identify and analyse well-defined engineering problems using codified standard methods.

PO-3: Design/ development of solutions: Design solutions for well-defined technical problems and assist with the design of systems components or processes to meet specified needs.

PO-4: Engineering tools, experimentation and testing: Apply modern engineering tools and appropriate technique to conduct standard tests and measurements.

PO-5: Engineering practices for society, sustainability, and environment: Apply appropriate technology in context of society, sustainability, environment, and ethical practices.

PO-6: Project management: Use engineering management principles individually, as a team member or a leader to manage projects and effectively communicate about well-defined engineering activities.

PO-7: Life-long learning: Ability to analyse individual needs and engage in updating in the context of technological changes.

COURSE OUTCOMES

After completion of the course, the students will be able to:

CO-1: Understanding material properties used for steel and RCC structures

CO-2: Application of design codes for steel and RCC structures

CO-3: Critical analysis of load and stress behavior in steel and RCC structures

CO-4: Design of steel beams and columns

CO-5: Design of RCC beams and columns

Course Outcomes	Expected Mapping with Programme Outcomes (1- Weak correlation; 2- Medium correlation; 3- Strong correlation)						
	PO-1	PO-2	PO-3	PO-4	PO-5	PO-6	PO-7
CO-1	3	-	-	3	2	2	2
CO-2	2	2	3	3	1	1	3
CO-3	1	2	2	2	-	1	1
CO-4	1	3	3	3	1	-	1
CO-5	1	3	3	3	1	-	1

GUIDELINES FOR TEACHERS

To implement Outcome Based Education (OBE) knowledge level and skill set of the students should be enhanced. Teachers should take a major responsibility for the proper implementation of OBE. Some of the responsibilities (not limited to) for the teachers in OBE system may be as follows:

- Within reasonable constraint, they should manoeuvre time to the best advantage of all students.
- They should assess the students only upon certain defined criterion without considering any other potential ineligibility to discriminate them.
- They should try to grow the learning abilities of the students to a certain level before they leave the institute.
- They should try to ensure that all the students are equipped with the quality knowledge as well as competence after they finish their education.
- They should always encourage the students to develop their ultimate performance capabilities.
- They should facilitate and encourage group work and team work to consolidate newer approach.
- They should follow Blooms taxonomy in every part of the assessment.

Bloom's Taxonomy

Level	Teacher should Check	Student should be able to	Possible Mode of Assessment
Create	Students ability to create	Design or Create	Mini project
Evaluate	Students ability to justify	Argue or Defend	Assignment
Analyse	Students ability to distinguish	Differentiate or Distinguish	Project/Lab Methodology
Apply	Students ability to use information	Operate or Demonstrate	Technical Presentation/ Demonstration
Understand	Students ability to explain the ideas	Explain or Classify	Presentation/Seminar
Remember	Students ability to recall (or remember)	Define or Recall	Quiz

GUIDELINES FOR STUDENTS

Students should take equal responsibility for implementing the OBE. Some of the responsibilities (not limited to) for the students in OBE system are as follows:

- Students should be well aware of each UO before the start of a unit in each and every course.
- Students should be well aware of each CO before the start of the course.
- Students should be well aware of each PO before the start of the programme.
- Students should think critically and reasonably with proper reflection and action.
- Learning of the students should be connected and integrated with practical and real life consequences.
- Students should be well aware of their competency at every level of OBE.

LIST OF FIGURES

LIST OF TABLES

TABLES OF CONTENT

1 DESIGN OF STEEL TENSION AND COMPRESSION MEMBERS

UNIT SPECIFICS

The chapter on the design of steel tension and compression members focuses on the fundamental principles and methodologies used to design structural components subjected to either tensile or compressive forces. It covers the concepts of stress, strain, and the material properties of steel, providing the necessary guidelines for determining the strength and stability of members like beams, columns, and rods. Students will learn to apply the relevant design codes and safety factors to ensure the structural integrity of steel members under various loading conditions. The chapter also highlights the importance of appropriate section shapes and sizes, considering axial loads and potential buckling effects in compression members.

RATIONALE

To design the steel tension and compression members, students must know the concepts of stress, strain, the material properties of steel, and the necessary guidelines for determining the strength and stability of steel members.

PRE-REQUISITE

Nil

UNIT OUTCOMES

The list of outcomes of this unit is as follows:

U1-O1: Understand different types of steel sections

U1-O2: Designing steel compression members

U1-O3: Designing steel tension members

Unit Outcomes	Expected Mapping with Course Outcomes (1- Weak correlation; 2- Medium correlation; 3- Strong correlation)				
	CO-1	CO-2	CO-3	CO-4	CO-5
U1-O1	3	2	-	2	-
U1-O2	1	3	3	3	-
U1-O3	1	3	3	3	-

1.1 INTRODUCTION

Steel is an iron-carbon alloy. In addition to carbon, incorporating minor proportions of manganese, sulphur, phosphorus, chromium, nickel, and copper can impart distinctive qualities to iron, facilitating the production of diverse steels. The impacts of various chemical components on steel are typically as follows:

- An enhanced concentration of carbon and manganese enhances tensile and yield strength but diminishes ductility, complicating the welding process.
- Excess sulphur and phosphorus exceeding 0.06 percent induce brittleness, adversely impacting weldability and fatigue strength.
- Chromium and nickel confer corrosion-resistant qualities to steel. It also enhances resilience to elevated temperatures.
- Incorporating a minor amount of copper enhances corrosion resistance.

Different varieties of steel are produced by making modest adjustments to the chemical composition, enabling their usage as structural members, tubes, pipes, sheets, strips, reinforcements for reinforced cement concrete, rivets, bolts, nuts, and welding applications. Steel structures are components shaped to a fundamental cross-section at a mill and subsequently processed to the required dimensions and configuration in a fabrication facility or at the construction site. A notable distinction between steel and concrete buildings is that the designer possesses greater control over the configuration of reinforced cement concrete components. In steel constructions, the designer is generally constrained to standard rolled sections. The extensive range of available steel pieces enables the attainment of any desired structural effect.

Steel possesses a high strength-to-mass ratio. Consequently, even for substantial constructions, the dimensions of steel structural components are minimal, optimising space in construction and enhancing visual appeal. It guarantees quality and exceptional durability. The rapidity of construction is a significant benefit of steel construction. Standard steel pieces can be prefabricated in the workshop or on-site, allowing them to be prepared in advance so that the structure can be erected promptly once the site is ready. Consequently, there is a significant reduction in building time. Steel structures can be reinforced subsequently if required. It requires the welding of extra parts. Steel constructions may be rapidly disassembled and relocated to different sites via bolted connections. The steel structures can also be utilised to construct water tanks.

Steel components exhibit a high strength-to-weight ratio. Consequently, a steel member with a diminutive cross-section and minimal self-weight can support substantial weights. Due to their lightweight nature, steel components may be easily managed and transported. Consequently, prefabricated components can be readily supplied. Well-maintained steel constructions have an extended lifespan. The characteristics of steel often remain stable over time. This renders steel the most appropriate construction material.

Steel, being a ductile material, does not experience instantaneous failure; instead, it provides apparent indications of imminent failure through significant deflections. Modifications and enhancements can be readily implemented in steel construction. Steel possesses the highest scrap value of all construction materials.

Steel structures are prone to corrosion. The maintenance expense is elevated due to the necessity of painting to avert corrosion. Steel components are expensive. Consequently, they necessitate regular painting. Steel structures require fireproof treatment, resulting in increased costs.

The design of steel structures entails purposeful planning, proportional member sizing for effective load bearing, and site erection considerations. The structure must fulfil its intended function, accomplished through effective planning. It must possess sufficient strength to endure direct and induced stresses over its lifespan. An insufficient evaluation of forces and their impacts may result in excessive deformation and failure. Consequently, structural design encompasses functional planning, an understanding of diverse stresses, material strength, and design methodologies. Furthermore, the structure must be cost-effective and straightforward to construct. An economic framework necessitates effectively utilising steel and both skilled and unskilled labour. While a minimum quantity of steel is typically attainable, using more steel can frequently yield savings if it produces a more straightforward structural configuration with reduced manufacturing requirements.

The design of a building comprises two components: (i) functional design and (ii) structural design. The initial phase involves designing the structure to meet its specifications, considering ventilation, illumination, aesthetic appeal, and other factors. The structural design involves proportioning building parts to ensure that loads are securely transmitted to the ground while minimising the usage of surplus material.

Try to find out!

Which members of the truss are being pulled apart (tension)?
Which members of the truss are being pushed together (compression)?
Are the vertical columns under compression due to the weight they support?
Are the diagonal braces under tension or compression?
Are the horizontal members of the truss in tension or compression?
How do the loads from the roof affect the columns?
Are the top chords of the truss bridge in compression?
Are the bottom chords of the truss bridge in tension?

1.2 PROPERTIES OF STRUCTURAL STEEL

The Bureau of Indian Standards has categorised structural steel according to its ultimate or yield strength. For instance, Fe 410 steel possesses a minimum tensile strength of 410 N/mm². The mechanical properties of steel are predominantly influenced by its chemical composition, rolling techniques, thickness, heat treatment, and stress history. Table 1 of IS 800-2007 defines several significant mechanical parameters of structural steel. The physical parameters of steel, regardless of grade, are presented in Table 1.1 (Clause 2.2.4 of IS 800-2007).

Table 1.1: Physical properties of structural steels

S. No.	Property	Value
1.	Unit mass of steel (ρ)	7850 kg/m^3
1.	Yield stress (σ_y)	220-540 N/mm^2
2.	Ultimate tensile strength	1.2 σ_y
3.	% Elongation (low carbon steel)	20
4.	Modulus of Elasticity (E)	2×10^5 N/mm^2
5	Modulus of Rigidity (G)	0.769×10^5 N/mm^2
6.	Poisson's ratio (μ)	
	(i) elastic range	0.3
	(ii) plastic range	0.5
7	Coefficient of thermal expansion	$\alpha_t = 12 \times 10^{-6}$/°C.

1.3 STRESS-STRAIN CURVE FOR MILD STEEL

Curve *OABC'CDEF* in Fig.1.1 illustrates the stress-strain relationship of a mild steel specimen under a progressively applied tensile load. The curve comprises several elements:

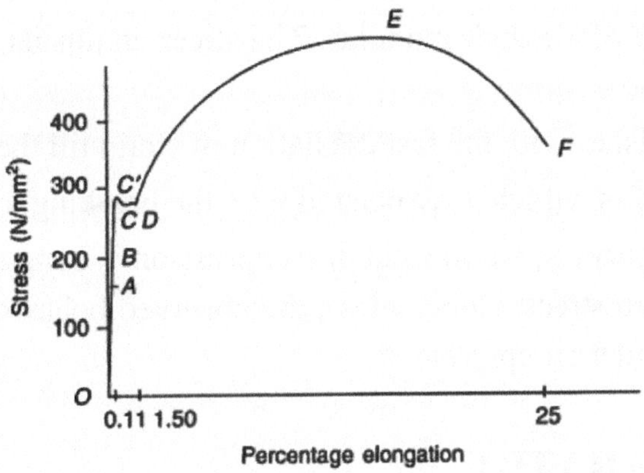

Figure 1.1: Stress-strain curve of mild steel

OAB denotes a linear relationship wherein the strain generated is proportionate to the applied stress, thereby adhering to Hooke's law.

A is the limit of proportionality, the stress at which linear variation terminates.

B denotes the elastic limit, the maximum stress at which a specimen returns to its original length upon removing the applied load. This tension is generally unmeasured, and *B* is presumed to align with *A*.

C'C denotes the upper and lower yield points, indicating the stress levels at which a distinct increase in strain occurs without any additional rise in stress. The stress magnitude at the upper yield point *C'* is contingent upon the specimen's cross-sectional geometry and the apparatus employed for testing. The upper yield point is often not achieved in several hot-rolled structural steel sections due to residual stresses resulting from the hot-rolling process. Therefore, it holds no practical relevance. The stress at the lower yield point *C* is the yield stress f_y, typically measuring 250 N/mm² for mild steel. The lower yield point is noted when the load is applied gradually. In the *OC* area, the material exhibits elasticity, and the slope *E* represents Young's modulus. The average value of *E* is 2×10^5 N/mm². The strain at yield stress is around 0.0012.

CD denotes plastic yielding, the strain that transpires post-yield point without a rise in stress. The strain at Point *D* of the plastic yield range is rather varied, with an average value of 0.014. Therefore, the strain inside the *CD* range is at least tenfold more significant than the strain at the yield threshold.

DE denotes strain hardening region, wherein increased stress results in augmented strain. The strain escalates rapidly with stress, culminating in the maximal load being attained. This segment of the schematic is currently not utilised for structural design.

E denotes the ultimate stress associated with the ultimate load. The initial slope of this region is approximately 4 percent of Young's modulus. The stress attains its maximum value, *E*, at a strain of no less than 0.2%.

From *E* to *F*, stress diminishes with the fast escalation of strain till the specimen fractures.

F denotes the breaking stress, which is associated with the breaking load.

The optimal stress-strain curve for mild steel in compression is congruent with that in tension until the point of maximum stress. Nonetheless, the observed behaviour diverges, suggesting a decreased yield stress under compression.

1.4 SLENDERNESS RATIO

The slenderness ratio (λ) is defined as the member of its unsupported length (l) and its minimum radius of gyration (r). While stiffness is not essential for the strength of a tension member, minimum stiffness is mandated by restricting the maximum slenderness ratio of the tension member. This limiting slenderness ratio is required to prevent undesirable lateral movement or excessive vibration.

$$Slenderness\,ratio\;(\lambda) = \frac{l_e}{r} = \frac{KL}{r} \quad 1.1$$

Where L = actual length of the compression member

$l_e = KL$, effective length

The maximum effective slenderness ratio values of a beam, strut, or tension member shall not exceed those in Table 3 of IS 800-2007.

The effective length KL is determined from the actual length L of the member, considering the rotational and relative translational boundary conditions at the ends. The effective length of KL can be determined using Table 1.2.

Table 1.2: Maximum values of effective slenderness ratios

S. No.	**Member**	**Maximum Slenderness Ratio (λ)**
1	A member carrying compressive loads resulting from dead loads and imposed loads	180

2	A tension member in which a reversal of direct stress occurs due to loads other than wind or seismic forces	180
3	A member subjected to compression forces resulting only from combination with wind/earthquake actions provided the deformation of such member does not adversely affect the stress in any part of the structure	250
4	Compression flange of a beam against lateral torsional buckling	300
5	A member normally acting as a tie in a roof truss or a bracing system is not considered effective when subject to possible reversal of stress into compression resulting from the action of wind or earthquake forces	350
6	Members always under tension (other than pre-tensioned members)	400

1.5 TYPES OF STEEL

Structural steel can primarily be categorised as mild steel and high-tensile steel. The requirements are outlined in IS 226-1975. In high-tensile steel, mechanical characteristics and corrosion resistance are improved through alloying with minor quantities of other elements or by augmenting the carbon content. According to IS 800-2007, the structural steel utilised in general construction must comply with IS 2062, which specifies weldable quality steel. Structural steel, excluding mild steel and high tensile steel, may be used if it meets weldable quality standards, provided that the permitted stresses and design specifications are appropriately adjusted and the steel is compatible with the chosen fabrication method.

1.6 ROLLED STEEL SECTIONS

Like concrete, steel sections of any configuration cannot be fabricated on-site due to elevated temperatures for melting and shaping the material. Standard-shaped, sized, and lengthened steel sections are produced in steel mills and sold in the market. The user must trim them to the specified length and utilise the necessary pieces for the steel framework. A variety of steel pieces are widely accessible in the market and are in high demand. These steel sections are referred to as Regular Steel Sections. Certain steel sections are hardly utilised; steel mills can manufacture them upon receiving orders. These steel components are referred to as special sections. Steel tables provide standard dimensions, weight per meter length, and geometric characteristics of different rolled steel sections. IS Handbook No.1 gives weight per unit length, geometric dimensions, and additional measurements for various steel sections, as Fig.1.2 illustrates.

1.7 STANDARD SPECIFICATIONS AND CODES

Standard specifications and codes are developed to ensure safe and cost-effective design, drawing upon historical design practices, empirical observations of existing structures, insights from failures, and research findings. The collected material is rigorously analysed, evaluated, and sanctioned by specialists before being disseminated in codes and standards. To this end, the Bureau of Indian Standards has issued various codes, standards, and handbooks, several of which will be often referenced and are enumerated below:

IS Handbook No. 1: Properties of Structural Steel Rolled Sections

IS 875-1987: Code of Practice for Design Loads for Buildings and Structures

IS 800-2007: Code of Practice for General Construction in Steel

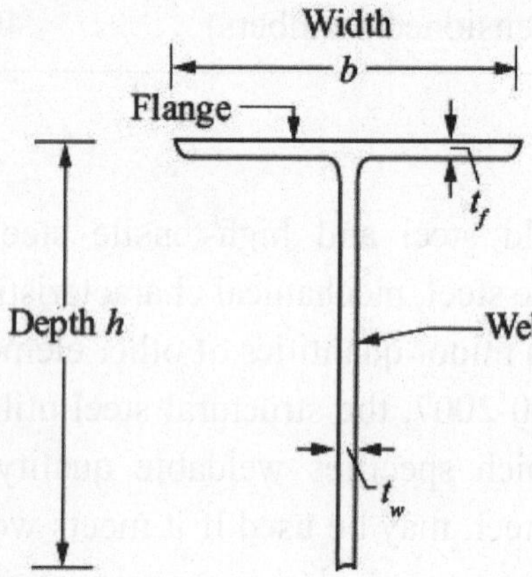

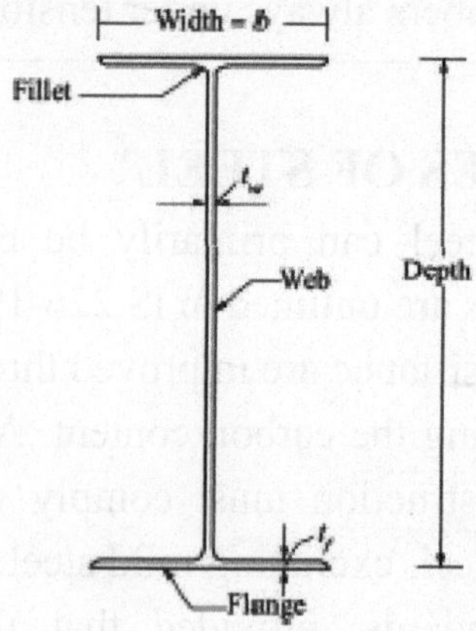

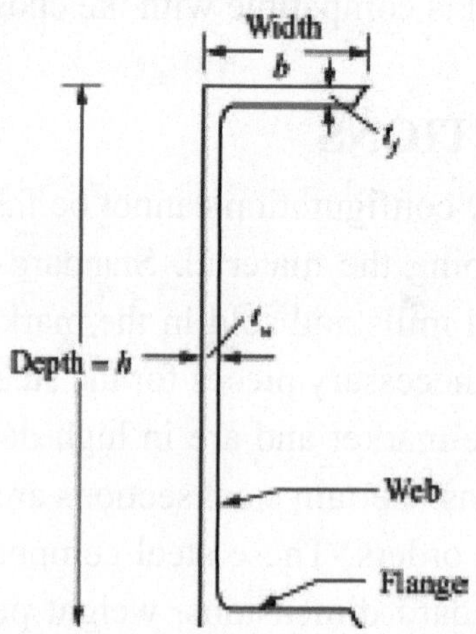

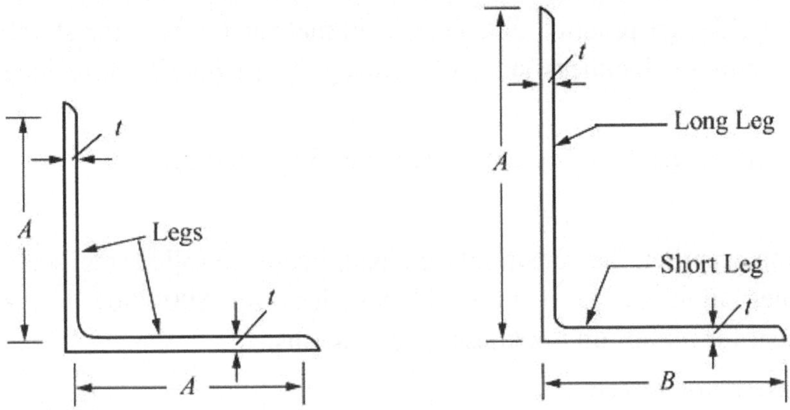

(a) Rolled steel equal angle. **(b)** Rolled steel unequal angle.

Figure 1.2: Rolled structural steel sections

A building code possesses legal authority and is enforced by a governmental agency. Building regulations do not provide design methodologies but delineate the standards and limits that must be met. Unlike building codes, design requirements provide more detailed direction for the design of structural components and their linkages. They provide the principles and criteria that allow a structural engineer to fulfil the requirements of a building code mandate. Special considerations are necessary in the steel design.

Dimensions and configuration

Steel is produced in steel mills and offered in specific dimensions. Therefore, the components of a steel structure must be designed using any accessible sections or a mix thereof. For instance, a beam section may be a conventional I-section or comprise built-up sections. The selection of a member's section is occasionally determined by the configuration of the adjacent member and the nature of the joint connecting the two members.

Buckling consideration

The allowable load per unit area in steel significantly exceeds the allowed values in concrete. Consequently, given an equivalent load, the cross-sectional area of a steel part is reduced. The slender components in a steel structure are susceptible to buckling under stress. The potential for lateral buckling in beams presents specific challenges. The stability of each component must be considered, as a steel member has multiple thin plates. To address the buckling problem, codes designate certain parts as ineffective.

Minimum thickness

Corrosion requires particular attention in steel design. Utilising extremely thin sections may lead to a small degree of corrosion, resulting in a significant percentage decrease in effective area. Consequently, design practice delineates minimal thicknesses for structural members. The following minimum thickness shall be utilised for members immediately exposed to weather:

- If completely accessible for cleaning and painting – 6 mm.
- If inaccessible for cleaning and painting – 8 mm.
- As mentioned earlier, the constraints are inapplicable to rolled steel sections, tubes, and cold-formed light gauge sections. Nonetheless, IS 800-2007 has eliminated the requirement for minimum thickness specifications.

Necessity for connection design

A steel design is incomplete without the design of the following connections:

- Connections among different standard sections chosen for a member.
- Interconnections among structural components (beams, columns, foundations, etc.).

Three prevalent types of connections are utilised:

- Riveted connections
- Bolted connections
- Welded connections

Nevertheless, the riveted connection is currently being abandoned. IS 800-2007 advocates for the utilisation of welded connectors. Bolted connections are necessary when different components are manufactured independently and joined on-site to provide the desired structure.

1.8 DESIGN PHILOSOPHY

The design seeks to determine the members' geometry, dimensions, and connection specifications to ensure the structure functions adequately during its intended lifespan.

- The structure must adequately support all anticipated loads with a suitable level of safety.
- Maintain deformations throughout and after construction.
- It should possess sufficient durability.
- It must possess sufficient resistance to overuse and fire.
- The structure must be sturdy and have alternative load routes to avert total collapse under unforeseen loading conditions.

The analytical design process involves idealising the structure, estimating anticipated loads, analysing to determine member forces, and sizing the members according to potential failure criteria. Due to constraints in accurately modelling the structure, operational conditions are maintained as a subset of the failure circumstances. The design principles employed are enumerated below in the sequence of their development, accompanied by concise explanations.

Working stress method

This is the most antiquated systematic analytical design approach. Although IS 800-2007 mandates limit state design, it allows for applying this strategy when limit state design is not easily implementable.

This philosophy assumes a linear stress-strain relationship up to the yield stress. To address uncertainties in design, acceptable stress is maintained as a fraction of yield stress; the ratio of yield stress to working stress is referred to as the safety factor. The members are designed to accommodate stresses within acceptable limits.

The subsequent load combinations are considered, and a 33% increase in acceptable stress is allowed when considering Dead Load (*DL*), Live Load (*LL*), and Wind Load (*WL*):

- Stress resulting from dead load (*DL*) and live load (*LL*) must not exceed the permissible stress.
- Stress resulting from dead load (*DL*) and wind load (*WL*) must not exceed permissible stress.
- Stress resulting from dead load (*DL*), live load (*LL*), and wind load (*WL*) must not exceed 1.33 times permissible stress.

Ultimate load method

The constraints of the working stress approach in evaluating true load-carrying capability prompted researchers to create the ultimate load method, commonly called the load factor method (LFM). The application of this philosophy to steel constructions is referred to as the plastic design method. In this procedure, a portion is considered to have developed a plastic hinge when all fibres yield. Subsequently, it continues to bear load, forming a plastic hinge, although it will not withstand any additional load. Nonetheless, the structure persists in withstanding further load until adequate plastic hinges are produced to create a collapse mechanism. This method implements safety precautions by proposing a load factor: the ratio of design load to working load. The recommended load factors conform to IS 800-1984.

Limit state method

It is an all-encompassing approach that addresses strength and serviceability criteria. IS 800-2007 advocates for the extensive application of this method and confines the working stress method to instances where the limit state method is inapplicable.

In the limit state method, the structural strength is evaluated until the emergence of the collapse mechanism. To address the uncertainties inherent in study, design, and construction, the code recommends augmenting working loads (derived from statistical analysis and referred to as characteristic loads) by partial safety factors, designating them as design loads. Nonetheless, it is essential to address serviceability requirements. Occasionally, it may be necessary to modify the design to meet serviceability standards.

1.9 TENSION MEMBERS

These structural elements subjected to direct axial tensile loads cause the members to elongate. A member under pure tension can be subjected to stress levels at or exceeding the yield limit without experiencing local or total buckling. Consequently, their design is unaffected by the classification of sections, including compact, semi-compact, and others.

Tension members transmit loads optimally as the entire cross-section experiences homogeneous stress. Numerous parameters, including connection length, fastener dimensions, spacing, net cross-sectional area, fabrication type, connection eccentricity, and shear lag at the terminal connection, affect the strength of these elements.

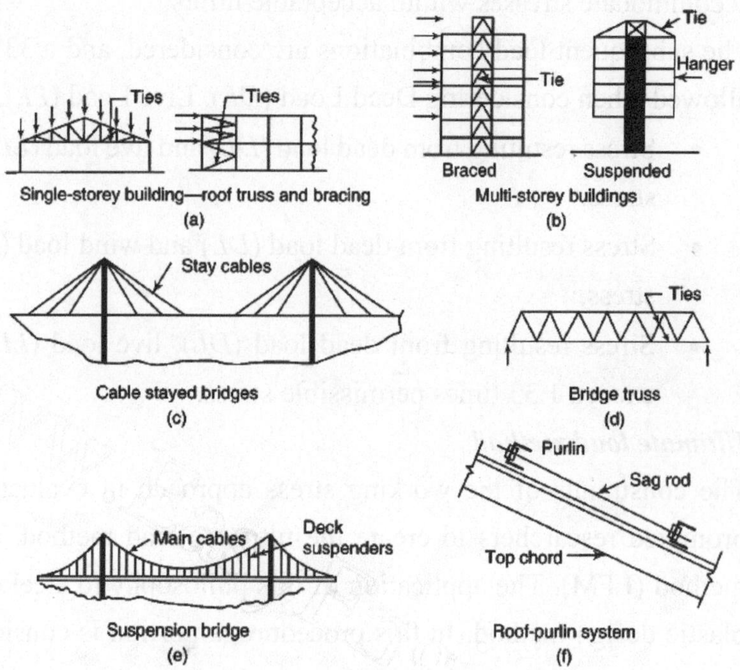

Figure 1.3: Tension members

Tension members are integral components of trusses (such as the bottom chord of roof trusses), bridges, transmission lines, communication towers, and wind bracing systems in multi-story buildings (Fig.1.3). Certain loading scenarios may induce tension in specific truss web members and tower components. They may undergo compression under alternative loading scenarios. Steel cables employed in suspension bridges and cable-supported roofs exemplify tension members. These cables are utilised in guyed towers and power line poles where alignment modifications occur.

1.10 TYPES OF SECTIONS USED FOR TENSION MEMBERS

Tension members may have a singular structural shape or be constructed from multiple structural shapes. Fig.1.4 illustrates the cross-section of many typical tension members. When two elements, such as angles, function as a single unit, they must be coupled at appropriate intervals to facilitate their collective operation as one entity. Single-angle or double-angle members are affixed to a single gusset plate at each extremity or may be welded directly to the webs or flanges of T- or I-chord components.

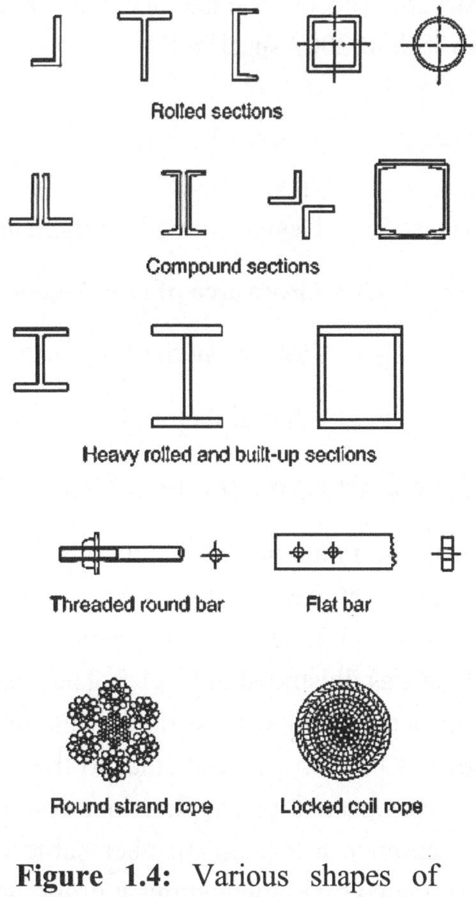

Figure 1.4: Various shapes of commonly used tension members

Structural T-sections can serve as chord members in lightly loaded trusses, replacing the back-to-back two-angle sections. The stem of the T-sections can join single or double-angle web members, thereby obviating the need for gusset plates, particularly in welded connections. Tubular members are utilised in roof trusses as stress components.

I-sections, channel sections, and built-up sections utilising angles and channels are employed where enhanced rigidity is necessary, particularly in bridge constructions.

Rods and bars serve as tension members within bracing systems. Sag rods support purlins, reinforce girts in industrial structures, or as longitudinal connections. They are either welded to the gusset plates or directly threaded and attached to the main members using nuts. When rods serve as wind bracings, they are pre-tensioned to mitigate the impact of sway.

1.11 DESIGN STRENGTH OF A TENSION MEMBER

The design strength of a tension member is the lowest of the following:

1.11.1 Design Strength Due to Yielding of Gross Section

A tension member without bolt holes can withstand the ultimate load without experiencing failure. Nonetheless, such a member will undergo significant deformation in the longitudinal direction (about 10%-15% of its original length) before fracture. At significant deformation, a structure becomes unserviceable. Therefore, the code restricts design strength, as Clause 6.2 of IS 800-2007 specified:

$$T_{dg} = \frac{A_g f_y}{\gamma_{mo}} \quad 1.2$$

where T_{dg} = Design strength of the tension member

A_g = Gross area of cross-section

f_y = Yield strength of the material

γ_{mo} = Partial factor of safety for failure in tension member by yielding = 1.1

1.11.2 Design Strength Due to Rupture of Critical Section

A tension member frequently attaches to the primary or other elements using bolts or welds. Tension elements coupled with bolts possess holes, resulting in a diminished cross-section known as the net area. Perforations in the members induce stress concentration under service loads, as illustrated in Fig.1.5. The tensile stress near a hole will be approximately two to three times the average stress on the net area, contingent upon the ratio of the hole's diameter to the plate's breadth perpendicular to the stress vector. Stress concentration is particularly critical when repeated load applications could result in fatigue failure or when there is a risk of brittle fracture in a tension member subjected to dynamic pressures. Stress concentration can be mitigated by implementing appropriate joint and member specifications.

When a tension member containing a hole is subjected to static loading, the region next to the hole initially attains the yield stress f_y. Upon additional loading, the stress at that location remains constant at the yield stress, whereas each fibre distant from the hole progressively attains the yield stress (refer to Fig.1.5(b)). Deformations persist with escalating load until the member ultimately ruptures (tension failure) when the total net cross-section attains the ultimate stress f_u.

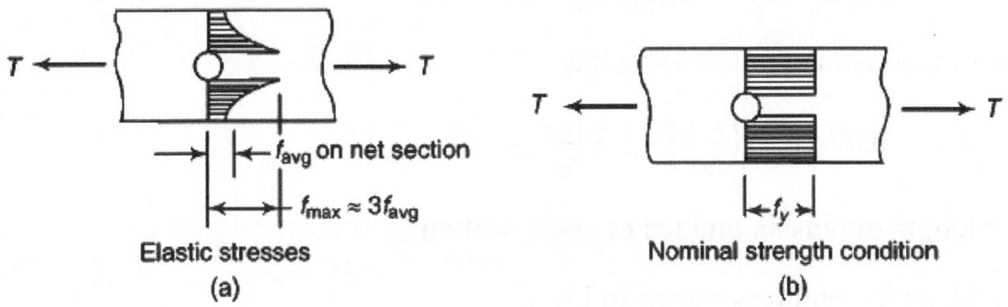

Figure 1.3: Stress concentration due to hole

The design strength resulting from net section rupture for plates is specified in Clause 6.3.1 of IS 800-2007 of the code:

$$T_{dn} = \frac{0.9A_n f_u}{\gamma_{m1}} \quad 1.3$$

Where f_u = Ultimate strength of the material

γ_{m1} = Partial safety factor for failure due to rupture of cross-section (= 1.25)

A_n = Net effective area of the cross-section, which is given by

$$A_n = [b - nd_h + \sum_i \frac{P_{si}^2}{4g_i}]t \quad 1.4$$

Where b, t = width and thickness of the plate respectively,

d_h = diameter of the bolt hole (2 mm in addition to the diameter of the hole in case the directly punched holes)

g = gauge length between the bolt holes

P_s = staggered-pitch length between the line of bolt holes

n = number of bolt holes in the critical section

I = subscript for summation of all the inclined legs

For the angle section, the design strength due to the rupture of the net section is given by:

$$T_{dn} = \frac{0.9A_{nc} f_u}{\gamma_{m1}} + \frac{\beta A_{go} f_y}{\gamma_{m0}} \quad 1.5$$

Where A_{nc} = Net area of the connected leg

A_{go} = Gross area of outstanding leg

$$\beta = 1.4 - 0.076\left(\frac{W}{t}\right)\left(\frac{f_y}{f_u}\right)\frac{b_s}{L_c} \leq \frac{f_u \gamma_{mo}}{f_y \gamma_{m1}} \geq 0.7$$

W = length of outstanding led of angle section

b_s = Shear lag width as shown in Fig.1.6

t = Thickness of the leg

L_c = Length of end connection

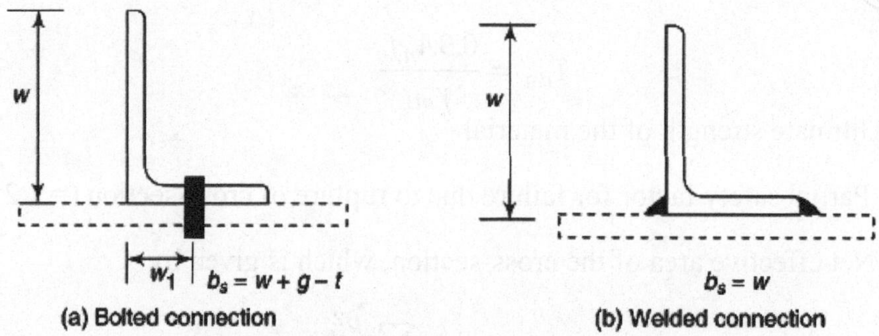

Figure 1.4: Angles as a tension member

For preliminary design purposes, the IS code recommend:

$$T_{dn} = \frac{\alpha A_n f_u}{\gamma_{m1}} \qquad 1.6$$

Where α = 0.6 when the number of bolts ≤ 2

= 0.7 when the number of bolts = 3

= 0.8 when the number of bolts is ≥ 4

= 0.8 for welds

1.11.3 Design Strength Due to Block Shear

The member's failure occurs along a trajectory characterised by tension on one plane and shear on a perpendicular plane at the fasteners, as illustrated in Fig.1.7. As seen in Fig.1.8(a), the gusset plate may experience tensile failure on the net area of section a-a. At the same time, in

Fig.1.8(c), it may fail on the gross area of section a-a. The angle member depicted in Fig.1.8(a) may detach from the gusset plate due to shear on net region 1-2 in conjunction with tension on net area 2-2, as seen in Fig.1.8(b). A comparable fracture of the welded joint depicted in Fig.1.8(c) is illustrated in Fig.1.8(d). The fracture of a gusset plate for a double-angle member or one of the gusset plates for an I-section is depicted in Fig.1.8(f). The gusset plate depicted in Fig.1.8(d) may likewise experience failure at the net section a-a. All these failures [Fig.1.8(b), (d), and (f)] are classified as block shear failures. The block shear phenomenon may occur as a form of failure when the material's bearing strength and the bolt's shear strength are elevated. The correct model for block shear failure involves the rupture of the net tension plane (BC) and the yielding of the gross shear plane (AB and CD), as illustrated in Fig.1.8(f), leading to the failure of the shear plane as the connection lengths decrease.

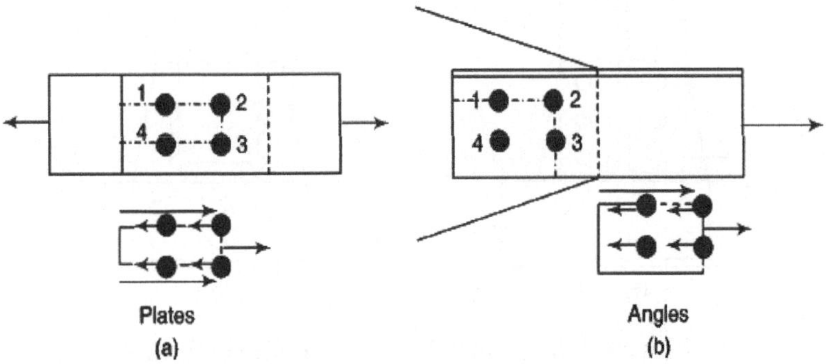

Figure 1.5: Block shear failure

Clause 6.4.1 of IS 800-2007 gives the block shear strength. The block shear strength of the connection is taken as the smaller of,

$$T_{db} = \frac{A_{vg} f_y}{\sqrt{3}\gamma_{m0}} + \frac{0.9 A_{tn} f_u}{\gamma_{m1}} \quad 1.7$$

$$T_{db} = \frac{0.9 A_{vn} f_u}{\sqrt{3}\gamma_{m1}} + \frac{A_{tg} f_y}{\gamma_{m0}} \quad 1.8$$

Where A_{vg} and A_{vn} = Minimum gross and net area in shear

A_{tg} and A_{tn} = Minimum gross and net area in tension

γ_{m0} = Partial factor of safety for failure in tension member by yielding = 1.1

γ_{m1} = Partial safety factor for the material strength governed by ultimate stress = 1.25

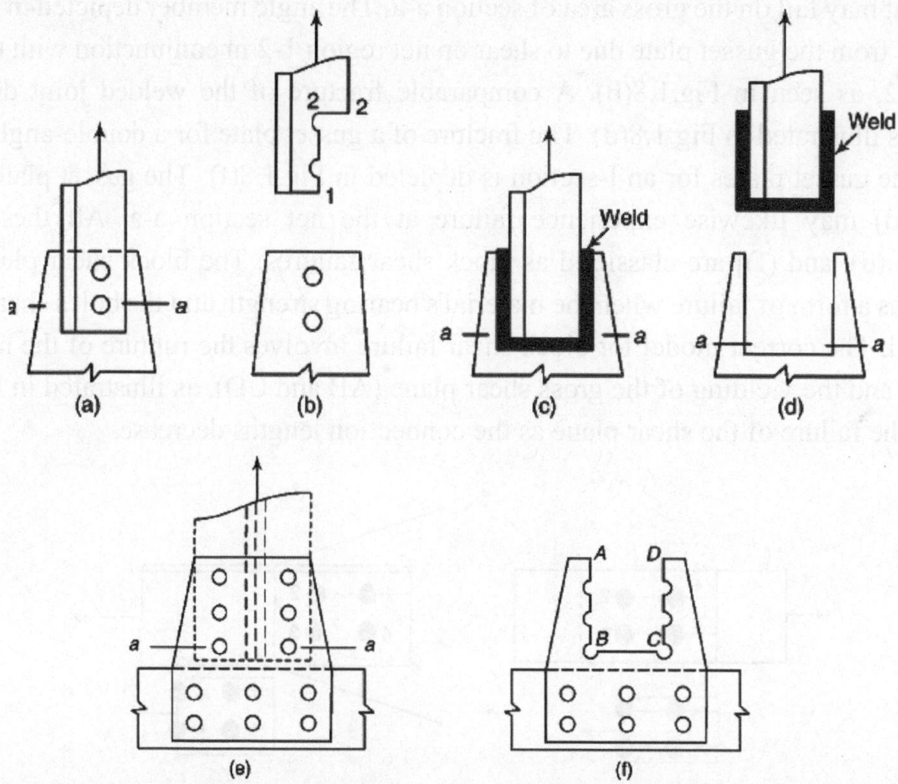

Figure 1.6: Example of block shear failure

Illustration 1.1: Determine the design tensile strength of plate 150 mm × 10 mm size with holes for the diameter of bolts 20 mm. The yield and ultimate stress of steel used are 250 MPa and 410 MPa, respectively.

Solution:

The strength of the plate will be a minimum of the following:

I. Yielding of gross section (T_{dg})

$$T_{dg} = \frac{A_g f_y}{\gamma_{mo}} = \frac{1500 \times 10 x 250}{1.1} = 340.91 \text{ kN}$$

II. Rupture of critical section (T_{dn})

$$T_{dn} = \frac{0.9 A_n f_u}{\gamma_{m1}} = \frac{0.9x1060x410}{1.25} = 312.912 \text{ kN}$$

Net effective area:

$$A_n = [b - nd_h + \sum_i \frac{P_{si}^2}{4g_i}]t$$

$$= [150- 2x22 + 0] \text{ x } 10 = 1060 \text{ mm}^2$$

III. Block shear strength (T_{db})

Gross area in shear (A_{vg}) = (60+35) x 10 = 950 mm^2
Net area in shear (A_{vn}) = (60 + 35 – 1.5 x 22) x 10 = 620 mm^2 (1.5 bolt holes are getting intercepted in shear area)
Gross area in tension (A_{tg}) = 45 x 10 = 450 mm^2
Net area in tension (A_{tn}) = 45 – 0.5 x 22) x 10 = 340 mm^2

Block shear strength is a minimum of the following:

$$T_{db1} = \frac{A_{vg} f_y}{\sqrt{3}\gamma_{mo}} + \frac{0.9 A_{tn} f_u}{\gamma_{m1}}$$

$$T_{db1} = \frac{950x250}{\sqrt{3}\, x\ 1.1} + \frac{0.9x340x410}{1.25} = 225.02 \text{ kN}$$

$$T_{db2} = \frac{0.9 A_{vn} f_u}{\sqrt{3}\gamma_{m1}} + \frac{A_{tg} f_y}{\gamma_{mo}}$$

$$T_{db2} = \frac{0.9x620x410}{\sqrt{3}x1.25} + \frac{450x250}{1.1} = 207.94 \text{ kN}$$

Therefore, T_{db} = 207.94kN

Hence, the strength of the plate is a minimum of

T_{dg}, T_{dn}, T_{db} = 207.94 kN

Illustration 1.2: An unequal angle ISA 100x75x8 is connected to a 12 mm gusset plate at the end with four numbers 16 mm diameter bolts. The angle is to be used as a tension member. Find the design tensile strength of the angle if the 100 mm leg is connected to the gusset plate. Use Fe 410.

Solution:

The strength of the plate will be a minimum of the following:

I. Yielding of gross section (T_{dg})

For ISA 100x75x8, A_g = 1336 mm^2 (See Table IV, SP:6(1)-1964)

$$T_{dg} = \frac{A_g f_y}{\gamma_{mo}} = \frac{1336 \ x \ 250}{1.1} = 303.64 \text{ kN}$$

II. Rupture of critical section (T_{dn})

Net area of connected leg: A_{nc} = (100-8/2-18) x 8 = 624 mm^2

Gross area of outstanding leg: A_{go} = (75-8/2) x 8 = 568 mm^2

$$\beta = 1.4 - 0.076\left(\frac{W}{l}\right)\left(\frac{f_y}{f_u}\right)\frac{b_s}{L_c} = 1.4 - 0.076\left(\frac{75}{8}\right)\left(\frac{250}{410}\right)\left(\frac{75+50-8}{150}\right) = 1.06$$

$$T_{dn} = \frac{0.9A_{nc}f_u}{\gamma_{m1}} + \frac{\beta A_{go}f_y}{\gamma_{m0}} = \frac{0.9x624x410}{1.25} + \frac{1.06x568x250}{1.1} = 321.04 \text{ kN}$$

Alternatively,

$$T_{dn} = \frac{\alpha A_n f_u}{\gamma_{m1}} = \frac{0.8[(624 + 568)x410]}{1.25} = 312.78 \text{ kN}$$

III. Block shear strength (T_{db})

Gross area in shear (A_{vg}) = [(3x50 + 35) x 8] = 1480 mm^2
Net area in shear (A_{vn}) = [(3x50 + 35) – 3.5 x 18] x 8 = 976 mm^2
Gross area in tension (A_{tg}) = 50 x 8 = 400 mm^2
Net area in tension (A_{tn}) = (40 – 0.5 x 18) x 8 = 248 mm^2

Block shear strength is minimum of the following:

$$T_{db1} = \frac{A_{vg}f_y}{\sqrt{3}\gamma_{mo}} + \frac{0.9A_{tn}f_u}{\gamma_{m1}}$$

$$T_{db1} = \frac{1480x250}{\sqrt{3} \ x \ 1.1} + \frac{0.9x248x410}{1.25} = 267.41 \text{ kN}$$

$$T_{db2} = \frac{0.9A_{vn}f_u}{\sqrt{3}\gamma_{m1}} + \frac{A_{tg}f_y}{\gamma_{mo}}$$

$$T_{db2} = \frac{0.9x410x976}{\sqrt{3}x1.25} + \frac{400x250}{1.1} = 257.25 \text{ kN}$$

Therefore, $T_{db} = 257.25$ kN

Hence, the strength of the angle is a minimum of T_{dg}, T_{dn}, $T_{db} = 257.25$ kN.

1.12 DESIGN OF A TENSION MEMBER

In designing a tension member, the designer must determine the type and size of the member based on the tensile force exerted on it. The selection of a member type is determined by the structural configuration and the member's location (e.g., double angles for the bottom chord or rafters in roof trusses, angles or pipes for web members in roof trusses, etc.). The design is iterative, encompassing the selection of a trial segment and an evaluation of its capacity. The subsequent steps are as follows:

1. The net area necessary, A_n, to support the design load. T is derived from the Eq. 1.9:

$$A_n = \frac{T_u}{f_u \gamma_{m1}} \qquad 1.9$$

2. The gross area can be calculated from the needed net area by augmenting it by approximately 25% to 40%. The required gross area may also be verified based on the yield strength of the gross section as follows.

$$A_g = \frac{T_u}{f_y \gamma_{m0}} \qquad 1.10$$

3. The quantity of bolts or welding necessary for the connections is determined. The items are organised in an appropriate configuration, and the total area of the selected part is computed. The design strength of the trial section is assessed using Eq. 1.6 and 1.7 for plates and threaded bars and using Eq. 1.8 and 1.9 for angles.

4. If the design strength is insufficient or excessive relative to the design force, a new trial section is selected, and Step 3 is reiterated until an acceptable design is achieved.

The slenderness ratio of the member is verified according to Table 3 of IS 800-2007.

Illustration 1.3: Design a diagonal tension member for a bridge to support a factored tensile load of 240 kN. The diagonal has a length of 3 m. It is connected to a 16 mm thick gusset plate using a single row of 20 mm diameter bolts of grade 8.8. Select an appropriate angle section for the member, considering grade 410 steel.

Solution:

For Fe 410, f_u =410 MPa and f_y = 250 MPa

For bolt of grade 8.8, ultimate tensile stress f_{ub} = 830 MPa, for d > 16 mm.

For a 20 mm diameter bolt, the stress area of bolt (A_{nb}) = 245 mm^2

Assuming the thread is to be included in the shear plane,

Shear strength of bolt = $\frac{F_{ub}}{\sqrt{3}\gamma_{mb}} A_{nb} = \frac{830x245}{\sqrt{3}x1.25} = 9392$ kN

Let the pitch of the bolt = 65 mm

End distance = 45 mm

Edge distance = 50 mm.

k_b = Minimum of $(\frac{e}{3d_o}, \frac{P}{3d_o}, \frac{F_{ub}}{F_u})$ = Minimum of $(\frac{45}{3x22}, \frac{65}{3x22}, \frac{830}{410})$ = 0.682

Design bearing strength of bolt = $\frac{2.5k_b d t F_u}{\gamma_{mb}} = \frac{2.5x0.682x20x8x410}{1.25}$ = 89.45 kN

(Assuming the thickness of the member section as 8 mm)

Therefore, no of bolts required = $\frac{240}{89.45}$ = 2.68 = 3 bolts (say)

Provide 3-20 mm diameter bolts.

Required net area based on net section rupture is given by,

$$T = \frac{0.9A_{nF_u}}{\gamma_m}$$

$$A_n = \frac{T\gamma_m}{0.9F_u} = \frac{240x1000x1.25}{410x0.9} = 813 \text{ mm}^2$$

This net area should be increased by 20% for getting gross area.

Gross area required = 1.2 x 813 = 975 mm^2

Required gross area on the basis of gross section yielding is given by,

$$T = \frac{A_g F_y}{\gamma_{mo}}$$

$$A_g = \frac{T\gamma_{mo}}{F_y} = \frac{240x1.1x1000}{250} = 1056 \text{ mm}^2$$

Try ISA 90 x 60 x 8,

Gross area, A_g = (90+60-8) x 8 = 1136 mm^2

Hole diameter, (d_o) = 22 mm

Net area of connected leg (A_{nc}) = (90- 8/2-22) x 8 = 512 mm^2

Gross area of outstanding leg (A_{go}) = (60 – 8/2) x 8 = 448 mm^2

Now, design strength due to net section fracture (T_{dn}) = $\frac{0.9A_{nc}F_u}{\gamma_{m1}} + \frac{\beta A_{go}F_y}{\gamma_{mo}}$

$$\beta = 1.4 - 0.076\left(\frac{W}{t}\right)\left(\frac{f_y}{f_u}\right)\frac{b_s}{L_c} \leq \frac{0.9\, f_u \gamma_{m0}}{f_y \gamma_{m1}} \geq 0.7$$

W = 60 mm

W_i = 50 mm

b_s = W + W_i – t = 60+50-8 = 102 mm

L_c = 2 x 60 = 120 mm

$$\beta = 1.4 - 0.076\left(\frac{60}{8}\right)\left(\frac{250}{410}\right)\left(\frac{102}{120}\right) = 1.104 \leq \frac{0.9\ x\ 410\ x\ 1.1}{250\ x\ 1.25} \geq 0.7$$

$$T_{dn} = \left(\frac{0.9x512x410}{1.25} + \frac{1.104x448x250}{1.1}\right) \text{ x } 10^{-3} \text{ kN} = 263.54 \text{ kN} > 240 \text{ kN}$$

Therefore, the member is safe in net section fracture.

Check for block shear:

A_{vg} = (2 x 65+45) x 8 = 400 mm^2

A_{vn} = (2 x 65 + 45-2.5 x 22) x 8 = 960 mm^2

A_{tg} = 50 x 8 = 400 mm^2

$A_{tn} = (50 - 0.5 \text{ x } 22) \text{ x } 6 = 312 \text{ mm}^2$

$$T_{db1} = \frac{A_{vg}F_y}{\sqrt{3}\gamma_{mo}} + \frac{0.9A_{tn}F_u}{\gamma_{m1}} = \left(\frac{1400x250}{\sqrt{3}x1.1} + \frac{0.9x312x410}{1.25}\right) = 275.8 \text{ kN}$$

$$T_{db2} = \frac{A_{tg}F_y}{\gamma_{mo}} + \frac{0.9A_{vn}F_u}{\sqrt{3}\gamma_{m1}} = \left(\frac{400 \; x \; 250}{1.1} + \frac{0.9 \; x \; 960x410}{\sqrt{3}1.25}\right) = 254.4 \text{ kN}$$

Therefore, Block shear strength (T_{db}) = Minimum of T_{db1} and T_{db2} = 254.4 kN.

Therefore, the member is safe in block shear.

1.13 COMPRESSION MEMBERS

Various philosophies are employed for a compression member based on its location inside a structure. The vertical compression elements of a structure that support flooring or girders are typically called columns. They endure substantial burdens. Vertical compression members are occasionally referred to as posts. The compression components utilised in roof trusses and bracing systems are called struts. They can be vertical or sloping and often possess short lengths. The upper chord components of a roof truss are referred to as the major rafters. The primary compression element in a crane is referred to as the boom. Short compression members located at the intersection of columns and roof trusses or beams are referred to as knee braces. Two of these compression members are shown in Fig.1.9.

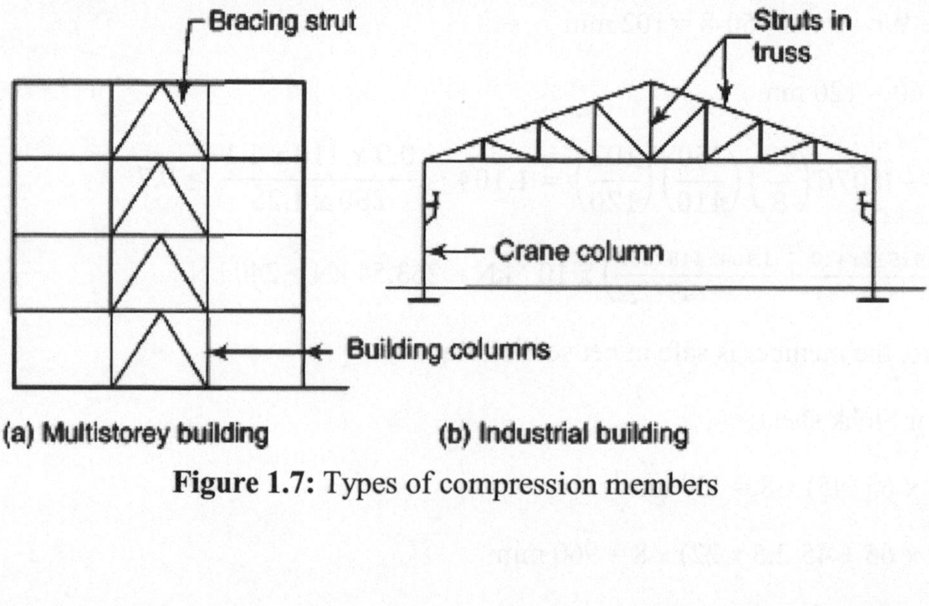

Figure 1.7: Types of compression members

1.14 SHAPES OF COMPRESSION MEMBERS

Commonly used compression members are shown in Fig.1.10. The design stress in compression members diminishes with a reduced radius of gyration; the section must be proportioned to achieve a maximum moment of inertia for the identical sectional area. This can be accomplished by focusing the region away from the section's centroid. The section should ideally maintain a consistent radius of gyration across all axes. This condition is satisfied by cylindrical tubes. Owing to challenges in establishing terminal connections, they were little utilised in the past. Increasing welding technique advancements have led to the increasing usage of tubular sections as compression members. The subsequent optimal configuration may be square tubing. ISHB sections are favoured as columns among the various sections due to their superior r values for equivalent cross-sectional areas. In built-up zones, reinforcement should be achieved by connecting plates to the flanges to enhance the r_{zz} value, which is inferior to the r_{yy} value (Refer to Table VI of SP 6(1)-1964). Angle sections are frequently utilised in roof trusses and transmission towers. Utilising equal angles rather than unequal angles as compression members is advantageous, as equal angles exhibit greater r_{min} values for identical cross-sectional areas.

1.15 BUCKLING CLASS OF CROSS-SECTION

Regardless of the designers' efforts to transfer the stress axially, the unforeseen eccentricity of the load is inevitable due to imperfections. This eccentricity induces a lateral bending moment, leading to bending compression. With the increase in axial compression, lateral deflection escalates, leading to heightened bending stresses. A state of instability occurs under a load significantly lower than the compressive strength of compression members. This occurrence is referred to as the buckling of columns. The propensity for buckling significantly diminishes the load-bearing capability of columns. The load-bearing capability is contingent upon the boundary conditions and the slenderness ratio of the column sections.

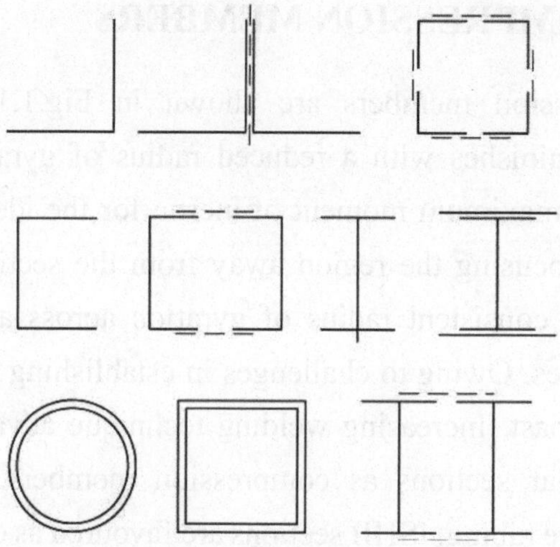

Figure 1.8: Various shapes of commonly used compression members

The cross-section of the compression members mainly influences the manufacturing imperfections that lead to unintentional eccentricity. The tendency to buckle varies due to such imperfections. Table 10 of IS 800-2007 categorises various cross-sections into four buckling classes: *a*, *b*, *c*, and *d*, as illustrated in Table 1.3.

Table 1.3: Imperfection factor, α

Buckling class	***a***	***b***	***c***	***d***
α	0.21	0.34	0.49	0.76

When an axially loaded compression part experiences overall instability (as opposed to local instability), it may bow in one of three distinct manners:

Flexural buckling

A deformation resulting from bending, or flexure, around the axis associated with the highest slenderness ratio. This often refers to the minor primary axis, characterised by the smallest radius of gyration. Compression members of any cross-sectional configuration may fail in this manner.

Torsional buckling

The aforementioned flexural buckling arises solely from bending; the sections are shifted from their initial location through translation without rotation. Thin-walled members with open cross-sectional geometries can exhibit weakness in torsion and may experience buckling through twisting rather than bending. Torsional buckling transpires when the torsional rigidity of the member is much less than its flexural rigidity. This failure type results from torsion around the member's longitudinal axis. It can occur just with doubly symmetrical cross-sections featuring exceedingly narrow cross-sectional elements. Standard hot-rolled shapes are not prone to torsional buckling; however, a member constructed from thin plate elements may be susceptible and should be examined.

Flexural-torsional buckling

This failure mode results from flexural and torsional buckling. The member flexes and rotates concurrently. This failure can occur exclusively in unsymmetrical cross-sections, including those with a single axis of symmetry—such as channels, structural tees, double angle forms, and equal-leg single angles—as well as those lacking any axis of symmetry, such as unequal-leg single angles.

1.16 DESIGN STRENGTH OF COMPRESSIVE MEMBER

The design compressive stress, f_{cd} of axially loaded compression members shall be calculated using Eq. 1.11:

$$f_{cd} = \frac{f_y/\gamma_{mo}}{\phi + (\phi^2 - \lambda^2)^{0.5}} \leq \frac{f_y}{\gamma_{mo}} \qquad 1.11$$

where $\varphi = 0.5\,[1 + \alpha\,(\lambda - 0.2) + \lambda^2]$

λ = non-dimensional effective slenderness ratio

f_{cc} = Euler buckling stress

α = imperfection factor, given in Table 7 of IS 800-2007

γ_{mo} = 1.1 for Fe 415 steel.

The design compressive strength P_d of a member is given by:

$$P_d = A_e f_{cd} \qquad 1.12$$

where A_e = effective sectional area, which is the same as gross area if bolt holes are filled with bolts. Deductions for bolt holes may be made only if the holes are not fitted with bolts.

For the benefit of users, tables are given in Table 9 of IS 800-2007 Table 9 to find design stress f_{cd} if $\frac{KL}{r}$ it is determined for all the four (*a, b, c* and *d*) classes of buckling.

1.17 DESIGN OF COMPRESSION MEMBERS

The subsequent procedures are standard in the design of compression members:

1. The design stress in compression is to be presumed.
2. The needed effective sectional area is $A = \frac{P_d}{f_{cd}}$.
3. Select a section to calculate the required effective area and r_{min}.
4. The end conditions and the type of connection dictate the effective length.
5. Determine the slenderness ratio, design stress f_{cd}, and load-bearing capacity P_d.
6. Amend the section if the computed P_d significantly deviates from the design load.

The design of compression members is conducted using a trial-and-error methodology.

Illustration 1.4: Design a single-angle discontinuous strut to carry a factored axial compressive load of 67 kN. The length of the strut is 3.0 m between intersections. It is connected to a 12 mm thick gusset plate by 20 mm diameter 4.6-grade bolts. Use steel of grade Fe 410.

Solution:

For steel of grade Fe 410: $f_u = 410$ MPa, $f_y = 250$ MPa

For bolts of grade 4.6: $f_{ub} = 400$ MPa

For 20 mm diameter bolts: $A_{nb} = 245$ mm^2

Partial safety factors for material: $\gamma_{m0} = 1.10$

$$\gamma_{mb} = 1.25$$

Let us assume the slenderness ratio to be 120. Corresponding to the slenderness ratio

$KL/r = 120$,

From the Table, design compressive stress is 83.7 MPa

Tentative area required, $A = \frac{67\times10^3}{83.7} = 800.477$ mm^2

From IS Handbook No.1, ISA 70 × 70 × 6 mm, providing an area of 806 mm^2, was selected. However, it failed (compressive strength was found to be 50 kN).

Next, let us try ISA 70 × 70 × 8 mm. From IS Handbook No.1, the relevant

properties of the section are, A = 1058 mm^2, r_v = 13.5 mm.

The effective length, $l = KL = 1 \times 3 \times 103 = 3000$ mm.

Let us provide 20 mm diameter bolts of grade 4.6 to make the end connections.

The strength of the bolt is single shear = $A_{nb}\, f_{ub}/(\sqrt{3}\ \gamma_{mb})$= $245 \times \frac{400}{\sqrt{3}\times 1.25} \times 10^{-3}$= 45.26 kN.

Strength of bolt in bearing = 2.5 $k_b d t f_u/\gamma_{mb}$ = $2.5\times20\times8\times\frac{410}{1.25} \times 10^{-3}$ = 131.2 kN

(let k_b = 1.0)

Hence, the strength of the bolt = 45.26 kN.

Number of bolts required for end connection = $\frac{67}{45.26} = 1.48 \approx 2$

Provide 2, 20 mm diameter bolts for making the end connections of the strut.

Considering the end fixity, connection factors from IS 800-2007,

$$k_1 = 0.2,\ k_2 = 0.35, \text{ and } k_3 = 20$$

The imperfection factor α = 0.49

$$\lambda_{vv} = \frac{\frac{l}{r_{vv}}}{\epsilon\sqrt{\frac{\pi^2 E}{250}}} = \frac{3\times\frac{10^3}{13.5}}{1\times\sqrt{\frac{\pi^2\times2\times10^5}{250}}} = 2.482$$

$$\lambda_{\phi} = \frac{b_1+b_2}{\epsilon\times(2t)\sqrt{\frac{\pi^2 E}{250}}} = \frac{70+70}{1\times\sqrt{\frac{\pi^2\times2\times10^5}{250}}\times(2\times8)} = 0.0985$$

$$\lambda_e = \sqrt{0.2 + 0.35 + 2.482^2 + 20 \times 0.0985^2} = 1.597$$

$$\phi = 0.5\times [1+0.49\times(1.597-0.2)+1.597^2] = 2.117$$

The design compressive stress,

$$f_{cd} = \frac{\frac{fy}{\gamma mo}}{\phi+(\phi^2-\lambda_e^2)^{0.5}} = \frac{\frac{250}{1.1}}{2.117+(2.117^2-1.597^2)^{0.5}} = 64.81 \text{ N/mm}^2$$

The design compressive strength,

$$P_d = A_e f_{cd} = 1058 \times 64.81 \times 10^{-3} = 68.57 \text{ kN} > 67 \text{ kN}$$

which is all right.

Illustration 1.5: Design a compression member with two back-to-back channels for carrying a 1200 kN load. The effective length of the channel is 5.6 m, and the yield f_y is 260 N/mm^2. The Area of each channel section is 5366 mm^2. Moment of inertia (M.O.I) of each section (I_{yy})= 4.706 x 106 mm^4, C_{yy}=24.4 mm.

Solution:

Given data P= 1200 kN.

Area of one channel section = 5366 mm^2.

So the area of 2 channel sections=2 x 5366= 10732 mm^2.

Permissible bending stress = S_{ac} = Load/Area= (1200 x 10^3)/10732= 111.82 N/mm^2.

Corresponding to permissible bending stress 111.82 MPa, slenderness ratio = 72.9.

$$\text{Slenderness ratio}(\lambda) = \frac{Effective\ length}{r_{min}} = 72.9$$

$$= \frac{5600}{r} = 72.9$$

$$r_{min} = 76.82 \text{ mm.}$$

So minimum moment of inertia = $I_{min} = (Ar^2) = 10732 \times 76.82^2 = 63.33 \times 10^6$ mm^4.

Let the spacing between the back-to-back of two channel sections be '*S*'.

The M.O.I of the combined section must be equal to the minimum M.O.I= 63.33 X 10^6 mm^4.

(I_{yy})combination= 63.33 x 10^6 mm^4.

$$2\,[\,I_{yy} + A(\frac{S}{2} + C_{yy})^2] = 63.33 \text{ x } 10^6 \text{ mm}^4.$$

$$2\,[(4.306\times 10^6) + 5366\,(\frac{S}{2} + 24.4)^2] = 63.33 \text{ x } 10^6 \text{ mm}^4.$$

S = 94 mm = Take 100 mm for simplicity in design.

So, the required spacing between the two channel sections is 100 mm.

Illustration 1.6: A tie member of a truss consists of a double-angle section of dimensions (80 mm x 80 mm x 8 mm) welded on both sides of a 12 mm thick gusset plate. Design a fillet weld to make the joint when the member is subjected to an axial tension of 270 kN.

Solution:

Let the weld lengths at the top and bottom edges be l_1 and l_2, respectively, for each angle.

So, the total length of the weld comes out to be = $2(l_1+l_2)$ mm

Maximum size of the weld (For square-edged connection) = (Thickness of thinner member-1.5) mm = (8-1.5) mm = 6.5 mm.

Minimum size of weld (Considering thickness of thicker member, i.e.12 mm) = 5 mm.

Let us provide a 5 mm weld size.

So, the strength of weld per mm length= $0.7\times 5 \times 108$= 378 N/mm

Strength of the weld=Tension in the member,

$378 \times 2(l_1 + l_2) = 270\text{x}10^3$

$(l_1+l_2) = 357.14$ mm

Now let us take a moment about the X-X axis, $378 \times 2\ l_1 \times 80 = 270 \times 10^3 \times 22.7$

$l_1 = 101.339$ mm.

So, $l_2 = 357.14 - 101.339 = 255.8$ mm.

So, provide $l_1 = 102$ mm and $l_2 = 256$ mm.

Illustration 1.7: Design a double-angle discontinuous strut to carry a factored load of 142 kN, resulting from a combination with wind load. The length of the strut is 3.0 m between intersections. The two angles are placed back-to-back (with long legs connected) and are tack-bolted. Use steel of grade Fe 410.

Angles are placed on opposite sides of the 12 mm gusset plate.

Angles are placed on the same side of the 12 mm gusset plate.

Solution:

For steel of grade Fe 410: $f_y = 250$ MPa

Let us assume a slenderness ratio of 110. The corresponding value of design compressive stress from Table 9(c) of IS 800-2007 is 94.6 N/mm^2.

Cross-sectional area required $= \dfrac{142 \times 10^3}{94.6} = 1501.057$

I. Angles placed on opposite sides of the gusset plate

From IS Handbook No. 1, select 2, ISA 65 × 65 × 8 mm (weight = 151 N/m).

Area provided = 1952 mm^2

Minimum radius of gyration, $r = r_z = 19.6$ mm

Effective length, $l = KL = 0.85 \times 3000 = 2550$ mm

$$\frac{l}{r} = \frac{2550}{19.6} = 130.10 < 250$$

For $\frac{Kl}{r} = 130.10, f_y = 250$ MPa and buckling curve c, the design compressive stress from Table,

$$f_{cd} = 74.22 \text{ N/mm}^2$$

The design compressive strength, $P_d = A_e f_{cd} = 74.22 \times 1952 \times 10^{-3} = 144.87 \text{ kN} > 142 \text{ kN}$

Provide 2, ISA 65 × 65 × 8 mm on opposite side of the gusset plate.

II. Angles placed on the same side of the gusset plate

Let us try the same angles ISA 65 × 65 × 8 mm, $A_e = 1952 \text{ mm}^2$

Minimum radius of gyration, $r = 19.6$ mm

$$\lambda = \frac{l}{r} = \frac{2550}{19.6} = 130.10 < 250$$

Effective length of the strut perpendicular to the gusset plate, $l = 1 \times 3000 = 3000$ mm.

From IS Handbook No. 1, for double angle section without any spacing (since it is on the same side of the gusset plate), the radius of gyration, $r = 28.8$ mm

Slenderness ratio, $l = 3000/28.8 = 104.17 < 130.10$

The critical slenderness ratio, therefore, is 130.10.

For $\frac{l}{r} = 130.10, f_y = 250$ MPa and buckling curve c, the design compressive stress from Table,

$$f_{cd} = 74.22 \text{ N/mm}^2$$

The design compressive strength, $P_d = A_e f_{cd} = 74.22 \times 1952 \times 10^{-3} = 144.87 \text{ kN} > 142 \text{ kN}$.

1.18 BUILT UP SECTIONS

To optimise value for a minimal radius of gyration without augmenting the section area, many elements are positioned distally from the significant axis, utilising appropriate lateral systems. The prevalent lateral systems are lacing or latticing and battening. Perforated cover plates provide this function as well. However, IS 800-2007 does not include any specifications for the design of such plates.

1.18.1 Lacings

Rolled steel flats and angles are used for lacing. One can use single-lacing or double-lacing systems (Fig.1.11). The purpose of implementing a lateral system is to separate the primary members of the column from the principal ones. The lacings experience shear forces due to horizontal forces acting on the columns.

IS 800-2007 delineates the subsequent regulations for the design of latticed columns. The latticing system shall be uniform to the greatest extent practicable. In the single-laced system, the orientation of lattices on opposing faces should mirror one another. It should not be contradictory. In bolted or riveted construction, the minimum width of lacing bars must be three times the bolt's or rivet's nominal diameter. The thickness of flat lacing bars must be no less than 1/40th of their effective length for single lacing and 1/16th for double lacing. Lacing bars must be positioned at 40° to 70° relative to the axis of the built-up member. The separation between the two principal members must be maintained to ensure $r_{yy}>r_{zz}$, where r_{yy} denotes the radius of gyration about the weaker axis and r_{zz} represents the radius of gyration about the stronger axis of each member (Fig.6.5 of SP 6(1)-1964). The maximum spacing of lacing bars must ensure that the slenderness of the main member between adjacent lacing connections does not exceed 50 or 0.7 times the most unfavourable slenderness ratio of the member. The lacing must be engineered to withstand a transverse shear Vt equal to 2.5% of the axial force in the columns. In two transverse parallel systems, each system must withstand shear forces. If the column experiences bending, V_t = bending shear + 2.5% of the column force. The effective length of a single-laced system is equivalent to the distance between the inner end fasteners. The effective length maybe 0.7 times the actual length for welded joints and double-laced connections at junctions. The slenderness ratio *KL/r* for lacing bars must not surpass 145. Laced compression members must include end tie plates. The effective slenderness ratio of laced columns shall be considered 1.05 times the actual maximum slenderness ratio to accommodate shear deformation effects.

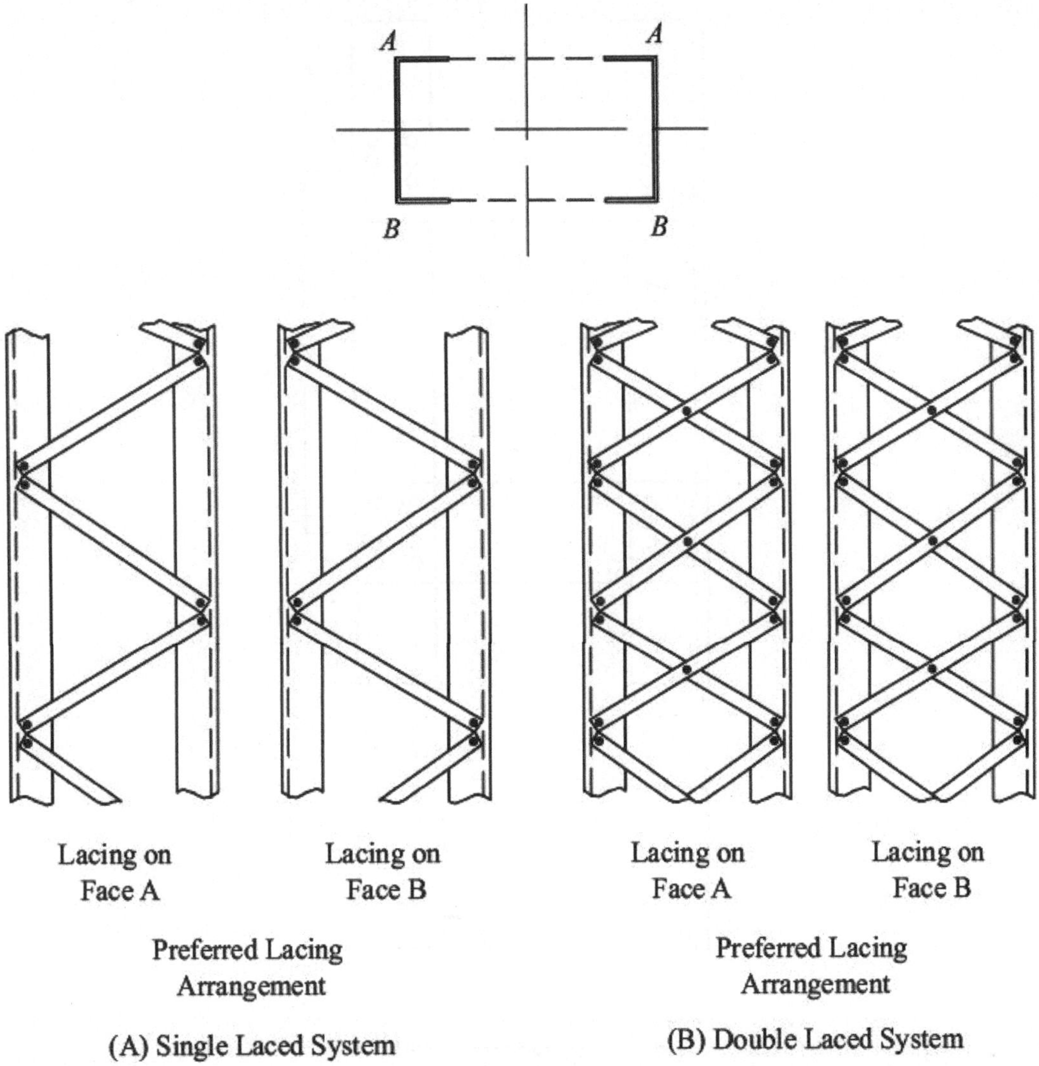

Figure 1.9: Laced column

1.18.2 Battens

Instead of lacing, one can use battens to keep members of columns at required distances. Fig.1.12 shows the use of batten plates.

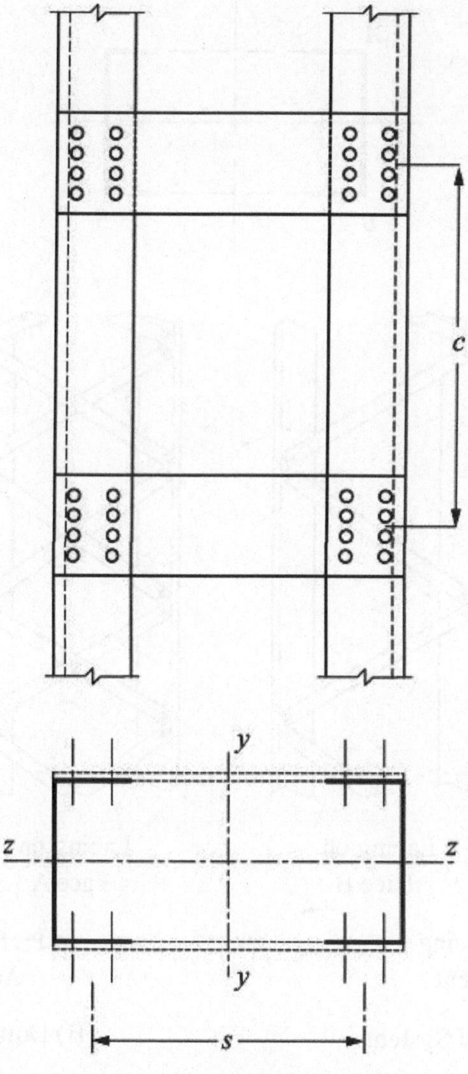

Figure 1.10: Battened column

IS 800-2007 delineates the subsequent regulations for setting battened columns. Batten plates must be installed symmetrically. Batten plates should be installed at both ends. They should be supplied at locations where the member remains inside its parameters. The quantity of battens must ensure that the member is partitioned into a minimum of three bays. They should be uniformly spaced and proportioned as much as feasible. Battens must consist of plates, angles, channels, or I-sections, and their ends shall be secured by riveting, bolting, or welding. Including battens ensures that the spacing between column members is regulated so that the radius of gyration around the axis perpendicular to the plane of the battens is not inferior to the radius of gyration about the axis parallel to the plane of the battens. The effective slenderness ratio of battened columns shall be considered 1.1 times the maximum real slenderness ratio of the column to accommodate shear deformation. The vertical spacing of battens, measured from the centre of one end fastening to the centre of the opposite end fastening, must ensure that the slenderness ratio of any column component over that distance does not exceed 50 or 0.7 times the slenderness ratio of the entire member about its *z-z* axis. Battens must be engineered to withstand the bending moments and shear forces resulting from a transverse shear force V_t, which is 2.5% of the total axial force. When columns are subjected to moments, the resultant shear force must be determined, and the design shear is the aggregate of this shear and 2.5% of the axial load. The design shear and moments at each connection for batten plates are provided by

$$V_b = \frac{V_t C}{NS} \, and \; M = \frac{V_t C}{2N}$$

where V_t= transverse shear force.

C = distance between centre to centre of battens longitudinally.

N = number of parallel planes.

S = minimum transverse distance between the centroid of the fasteners connecting the batten to the main member.

SUMMARY

Steel structural tension and compression members are designed to resist forces under load while maintaining structural integrity and stability. Tension members are governed by yield strength, cross-sectional area, and buckling risk, while compression members are complex and require evaluating critical buckling loads and effective length factors. Designing these members involves determining steel grades, analysing loads, checking for buckling risks, and adhering to IS 800-2007 safety, strength, and serviceability requirements.

EXERCISE

Make a few groups of students, each having five students. The students take on different roles in managing a construction project. Assigning each group a specific construction project scenario (e.g., building a tower, constructing a steel bridge, water tank). In their roles:

- Identify and discuss unique steel sections used in their assigned construction
- Determine why a particular steel section is utilised in the assigned construction
- Discuss the choice of tension and compression members based on their load distribution and construction feasibility.

MULTIPLE CHOICE QUESTIONS

1. Cables may be used effectively for which of the following structure(s)?

   A) Chimney

   B) Suspended

   C) Bridge

   D) All the above

2. The maximum slenderness ratio for tension members shall not exceed:

   A. 180

   B. 300

   C. 350

   D. 400

3. As per the code, the permissible stress in axial tension in N/mm² on the net effective area of the section shall not exceed (where f_y is the minimum yield stress of steel in N/mm²):

   A. $0.5 f_y$

   B. $0.6 f_y$

   C. $0.75 f_y$

   D. $0.8 f_y$

4. The maximum centre-to-centre distance between rivets in a tension member of thickness 10 mm is

A. 200 mm

B. 160 mm

C. 120 mm

D. 100 mm

5. A Tie member is a
   A. Tension member

   B. Compression member

   C. Torsion member

   D. Flexural member

6. The working stress (in N/mm^2) for structural steel in tension is the order of
   A. 15

   B. 75

   C. 150

   D. 750

7. Lug angles
   A. Are used to reduce the length of the connection

   B. Are unequal angles

   C. Increases shear legs

   D. All options are correct

8. In a tension member, if one or more rivet holes are off the line, the failure of the member depends upon
   A. Pitch

   B. Gauge

   C. Diameter of rivet holes

   D. All of these

9. The effective slenderness ratio of a column fixed at both ends is
   A. 0.5 L/r

   B. L/r

C. 0.65 *L/r*

D. 2 *L/r*

10. The slenderness ratio of a column is zero when its length:

A. Effective length is equal to the actual length

B. Is very large

C. is equal to its radius of gyration

D. Is supported on all sides throughout its length

11. The slenderness ratio is 180 for a circular column with its end hinged. The *1/d* ratio of the column is

A. 60

B. 40

C. 45

D. 35

12. The effective buckling length of a strut made of double angles back to back connected by bolting is:

A. 1.2 *L*

B. 0.7 *L*

C. 0.85 *L*

D. 1.0 *L*

13. For the same load, unsupported length and end conditions, a laced column as compared to a battened column:

A. Is weaker

B. Is stronger

C. Is equally strong

D. Cannot be compared

14. As per the code, the slenderness ratio of the lacing bars should not exceed:

A. 80

B. 100

C. 145

D. 225

ANSWERS TO MULTIPLE CHOICE QUESTIONS

1	2	3	4	5	6	7	8	9	10
D	D	B	B	A	C	A	D	A	D
11	**12**	**13**	**14**						
B	C	B	C						

SHORT ANSWER TYPE QUESTIONS

1. List some of the tension members used in buildings and bridges.
2. What are the factors that influence the strength of tension members?
3. List the type of cross-section that can be used as tension members and their use in typical structures.
4. How can the rods, which are used as tension members, be pre-tensioned?
5. Why are rods, which are used as tension members, required to be pre-tensioned?
6. What is the use of spacer plates or stitch plates? At what spacing are they connected to the members?
7. Write a short note on using ropes and strands in bridges.
8. Why is the capacity of a rope always less than the total capacity of wires put together?
9. What is the equivalent modulus of elasticity of ropes?
10. What is meant by the slenderness ratio?
11. Write down the expression for the axial elongation of the member subjected to a tensile force.
12. What is the main difference between a tension member's true and engineering stress-strain curves?
13. How is the yield point of a high-strength steel tension member determined?
14. List the different modes of failures of a tension member.
16. Write short notes on block shear failure in plates and angles.
17. Under what circumstances will the block shear failure be predominant?
18. Why are drilled holes preferred over punched holes?

19. By what methods can the effect of punched holes be considered in the design calculation?
20. Explain the different modes of failure of tension members.
22. What is a lug angle? Illustrate with a sketch. Why are lug angles used?
23. Write short notes on tension member splices.
24. State the parameters that affect the strength of compression members.
25. Define the effective length of a column.
26. How does strain hardening affect the strength of short columns?
27. What is inelastic buckling?

LONG ANSWER TYPE QUESTIONS

1. Design a single angle section as a tension member for a roof truss to carry a factored tensile force of 300 kN. The member is subjected to possible stress reversal due to wind action. The effective length of the member is 4 m. Use 16 mm diameter shop bolts of grade 4.6 for the connection.
2. Determine the tension capacity of a 150 x 90 x 8 mm angle in Fe 410 steel, assuming. Connection through the longer leg by two rows of four M22 bolts. A roof truss has a tension member with a length of 6 m. If the maximum load on the member is 50 kN, determine the required section size using IS 800-2007.
3. A steel tension member with a rectangular cross-section is connected to a gusset plate using four 20 mm diameter bolts. The effective net area of the member is 2250 mm². Steel yield strength is 250 MPa, and the ultimate strength is 410 MPa. Calculate the design tensile strength of the member as per the Limit State Method. Determine the safety factor if the applied load on the member is 400 kN.
4. A truss strut of 3.6 m length is connected at each end with welding to the gusset plate. The strut is of a section ISA 110 × 110 × 10 mm. Determine its equivalent slenderness ratio.

5. Design a single-angle strut carrying a factored compressive load of 90 kN with the length between the centre-to-centre intersection as 2 m. The design also supports the bolted end connections.
6. A single angle discontinuous strut ISA 70 x 70 x 8 is 1.5 m long. It is connected by one bolt at each end. Calculate the safe load that it can carry.
7. A double-angle discontinuous strut consists of two ISA 60 x 60 x 5 connected back-to-back to both sides of a 12mm thick gusset plate with two bolts. The length of the strut is 5 m. Calculate the section's safe load-carrying capacity.
8. Calculate the safe load over a compression member of an unsupported length of 5 m. The member is to be used in a transmission line tower. The ends are held in position but not restrained in direction. The overall section of the member is 190 mm × 190 mm. Use steel of grade Fe 410.
9. Calculate the value of the least radius of gyration for a compound column consisting of ISHB 250 @ 536.6 N/m with one cover plate 300 mm × 20 mm on each flange. Assume steel of grade Fe 410, bolts of grade 4.6, and load factor 1.5.
10. Design a compression member with two back-to-back channels for carrying a 1200 kN load. The effective length of the channel is 5.6 m, and the yield f_y is 260 N/mm^2. Area of each channel section= 5366 mm^2, Moment of Inertia of each section (I_{yy})= 4.706 x 106 mm^4, C_{yy}=24.4 mm.
11. Design a column of effective length 5.9 m. It is subjected to a factored axial compressive load of 1900 kN. Provide two back-to-back channels connected by battens and site-welded connections. Steel grade used Fe 410.

TUTORIAL

You are part of a team designing a truss bridge for a village near the river. The population of the village is 1500, having 100 vehicles. The rest are pedestrians or cyclists, and no heavy vehicle is present in the village. Determine:

- The forces in each truss member (tension or compression).
- The size of tension and compression members.
- The type of connections to be used (bolted or welded) and their specifications. Ensure the design adheres to IS 800-2007 standards.

KNOW MORE

For more information related to this topic, scan the QR code.

OR

Type this link in your browser

https://www.steel-insdag.org/assets/frontend/trmpdf/Chapter5.pdf

https://www.steel-insdag.org/assets/frontend/trmpdf/Chapter6.pdf

BIBLIOGRAPHY

1. Bureau of Indian Standards. (2000). IS 456:2000 - *Plain and Reinforced Concrete - Code of Practice* (4th Revision), New Delhi.
2. Duggal, S. K. (2014). *Reinforced Concrete Design*, Tata McGraw Hill Education: New Delhi.
3. Krishna Raju, and N. Pranesh, R.N. (2018). *Reinforced Concrete Design Principles and Practice*, New Age International: Mumbai.

4. Pillai, S.U., and Menon, D. (2017). *Reinforced Concrete Design*, McGraw Hill Publications: New Delhi.

5. Ramamrutham, S., & Narayanan, R. (2013). *Design of Reinforced Concrete Structures*, New Delhi: Dhanpat Rai Publishing Company.

6. Sinha N.C., and Roy S.K. (2007). *Fundamentals of Reinforced Concrete*, S. Chand & Co.: New Delhi.

7. Varghese, P. C. (2008). *Limit State Design of Reinforced Concrete*, Prentice Hall India Learning Private Limited: Delhi.

2 DESIGN OF STEEL BEAMS

UNIT SPECIFICS

In this unit, students will focus on the design of structural steel beams, beginning with understanding bending stresses using the bending moment equation and material properties to ensure the beam's strength under bending loads. The design of simple I and channel sections will be explored, where students will determine the appropriate dimensions and thickness to meet the design requirements. Additionally, the unit covers the critical check for shear strength as per IS 800-2007, ensuring that the selected beam sections can safely resist shear forces and bending stresses. This knowledge equips students with the tools to design and evaluate the structural integrity of steel beams in real-world applications.

RATIONALE

To design a safe and efficient structure, students must be able to calculate bending stresses, design simple I and channel sections, and perform shear checks by IS 800-2007.

PRE-REQUISITE

Basic mathematics

UNIT OUTCOMES

The list of outcomes of this unit is as follows:

U2-O1: Understand the standard steel beam sections

U2-O2: Design I and channel sections

U2-O3: Shear check for steel members as per IS 800-2007

Unit Outcomes	Expected Mapping with Course Outcomes (1- Weak correlation; 2- Medium correlation; 3- Strong correlation)				
	CO-1	CO-2	CO-3	CO-4	CO-5
U2-O1	3	2	1	2	-
U2-O2	1	3	2	3	-
U2-O3	-	3	3	2	-

2.1 INTRODUCTION

A beam is a structural element with a length much greater than its cross-sectional dimensions. It is subjected to lateral loads that induce bending moments and shear forces inside the member. Beams must be appropriately sized for bending strength, considering the local and lateral instability of the compression flange, and the chosen beam section must provide the requisite shear strength and bearing capacity. The beam section must be designed for stiffness, ensuring deflections and deformations remain within the limitations established for service load situations. The beam section must be designed cost-effectively by considering the grade of steel used for yielding. The beam material should be positioned as far from the neutral axis as feasible to maximise the moment of inertia in the beam section. The web area must be sufficiently large to provide acceptable shear resistance. Beam design is hampered by lateral buckling of the beam or buckling of the compression flange or web section. Another issue with beam design is the depth of the beam cross-section. Augmenting the beam's depth enhances its flexural resistance while diminishing its lateral or web buckling resistance.

Purlins are beams positioned between trusses that provide support for roof sheeting. Angles or channels are typically employed for this purpose. T-sections are utilised in water tanks to reinforce steel plates. I-sections are commonly used as beams in structures; I-sections with supplementary plates affixed to flanges are utilised for greater loads. Build-up sections, such as plate girders, are employed when more substantial sections are necessary.

There are primarily two categories of beams based on the lateral supports for compression flanges: (a) Laterally supported beams and (b) Laterally unsupported beams. If the compression flanges are laterally supported by flooring, they primarily experience bending and shear forces. If the compression flange of the beam lacks lateral support, lateral buckling of the flange diminishes the beam's load-carrying capacity. This chapter outlines the design of beams according to limit state considerations proposed by IS 800-2007.

2.2 PLASTIC MOMENT CARRYING CAPACITY OF SECTION

The flexural stress exhibits a linear variation within the elastic limit from the compression side to the tension side, as illustrated in Fig.2.1(Class 4). The load is progressively augmented, resulting in heightened fibre tensions, particularly affecting the extreme fibres. The load escalates until the outer fibres attain yield stress – Fig.2.1(Class 3). From the stress-strain relationship for steel it is clear that the strain hardening segment of the curve is disregarded, and it is assumed that upon reaching the yield point, fibres yield without providing any more resistance to load. According to the principle of plastic analysis, the severely stressed fibre, upon yielding, cannot resist any load or moment. Nevertheless, while the inner fibres remain unyielded, the extra stress is countered by the unyielded segment of the beam section. As the load incrementally increases, the internal fibres will yield and stop bearing any more load (Fig. 2.1(Class 2)). As the strain builds, the interior fibres that have not yet surrendered resist the weight. The resistance to load escalates until all the fibres give-up (Fig.2.1(Class 1)). When all the fibres have surrendered, the beam section provides no more resistance to the load. When all the fibres have surrendered at a segment, this state is called the creation of a plastic hinge. Upon reaching the plastic hinge condition, limitless rotation can occur at a constant force without resisting further load. The carrying capacity of the section at this ultimate load is referred to as the plastic moment capacity of the section (M).

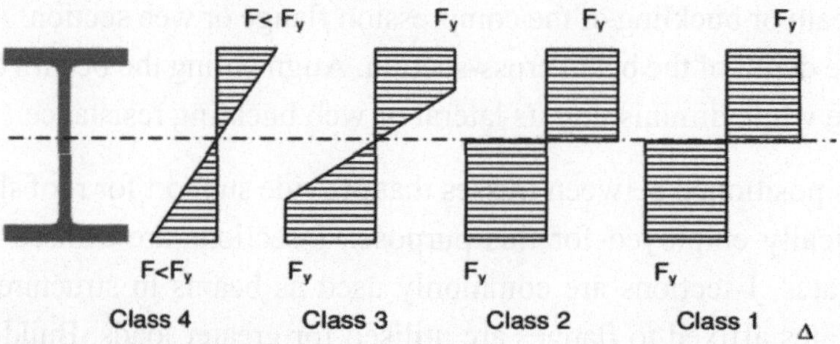

Figure 2.1: Plastic moment capacity of a beam section

For the beam section, as shown in Fig.2.1

Let A_c = Area of beam section in compression

A_t = Area of beam section in tension

A = Total area of beam section = $A_c + A_t$

Now Total compressive force (C) = $A_c f_y$

Total tensile force (T) = $A_t f_y$

For static equilibrium, $C = T$

$$A_c f_y = A_t f_y$$

Therefore

$$A_c = A_t = \frac{A}{2} \qquad 2.1$$

The stress in the beam portion varies from compression to tension. The location at which stress transitions to zero is termed the plastic neutral axis of the beam segment. Eq. 2.1 indicates that the plastic neutral axis bisects the beam section into two equal segments. The plastic neutral axis is located at the mid-depth of the section for symmetric sections. For asymmetrical sections (such as T-sections, L-sections, shown in Fig. 2.2), it must be determined based on the condition obtained in Eq. 2.1. The plastic moment capacity of the section can be determined by calculating the moment of horizontal forces about the plastic neutral axis. The moments resulting from compressive and tensile forces are cumulative.

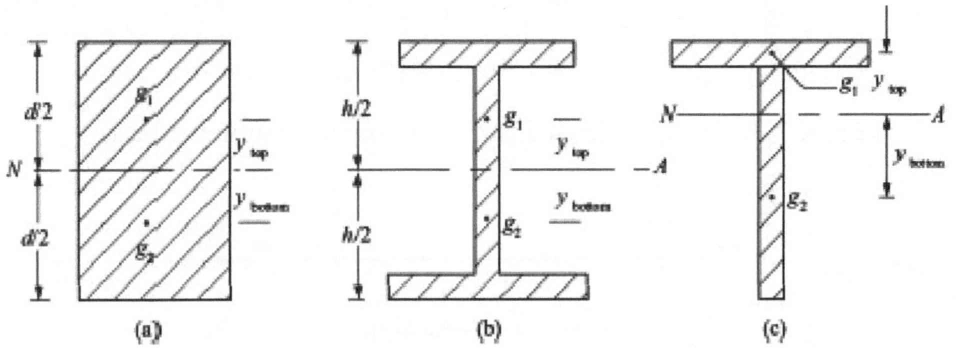

Figure 2.2: Plastic neutral axis

Let M_p = Plastic moment capacity of a section.

Then, from the bending equation, it can be deduced that $M_p = f_y Z_p$

Where f_y = Yield stress of the material of the beam section

Z_p = Plastic section modulus of the beam section

For standard rolled sections, Z_p is approximately 1.125 to 1.14 times Z_e for I-sections and about 1.7 to 1.8 times for channel sections. The collapse mechanisms of the propped cantilever and fixed beam are illustrated in Fig. 2.3 and 2.4, respectively.

2.3 CLASSIFICATION OF CROSS-SECTIONS

The limit state design of steel beams requires that sections be classified since the ultimate moment carrying capacity of the beam depends on the type of section being used, i.e., plastic, compact, semi-compact, or slender. These four section classes have been defined based on yield, plastic moments, and rotation capacities. The various types of sections are shown in Fig.2.5.

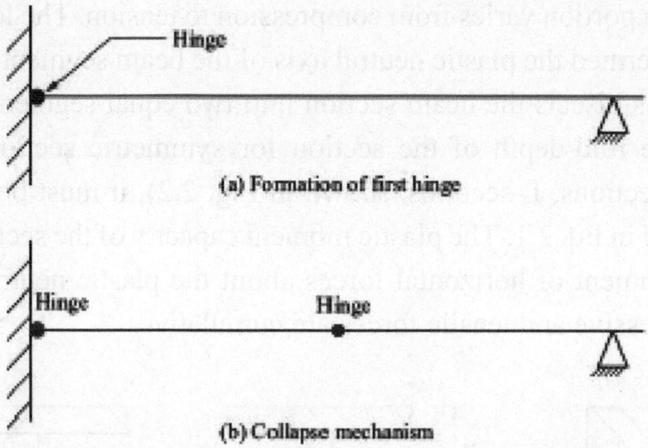

Figure 2.3: Collapse mechanism for a propped cantilever beam

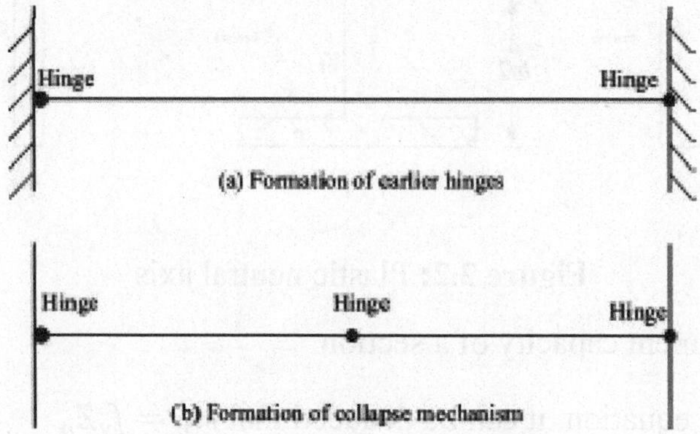

Figure 2.4: Collapse mechanism for a fixed beam

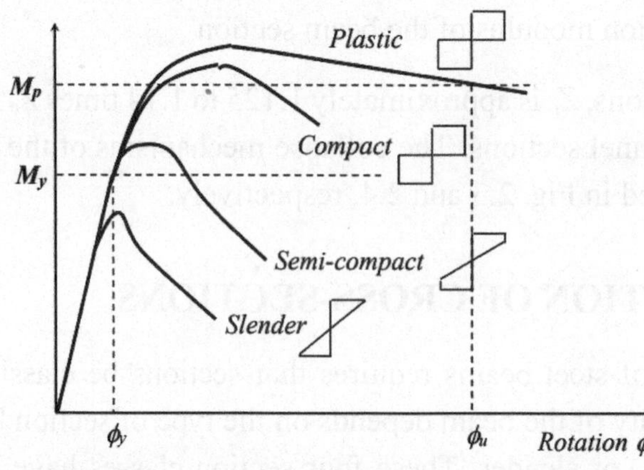

Figure 2.5: Moment rotation characteristics of four classes of cross-section

The steel beam design procedure selects a trial section, assuming it's a plastic Class 1, checks its bending, shear strength, and deflection, and revises it if necessary.

2.4 BENDING STRESS OF A BEAM

IS 800-2007 considers two cases, one with a design shear strength V less than $0.6V_d$ and the other with a V more than $0.6V_d$. When $\frac{d}{t_w} > 67\epsilon$, Shear buckling of the web will likely occur.

- Low shear case $V \leq 0.6V_d$

The design bending strength M_d shall be taken as:

$$M_d = \beta_b \frac{Z_p f_y}{\gamma_{m0}} \tag{2.2}$$

$$M_d \leq 1.2 \frac{Z_e f_y}{\gamma_{m0}} \text{ for simply supported beam}$$

$$M_d \leq 1.5 \frac{Z_e f_y}{\gamma_{m0}} \text{ for cantilever beam}$$

Where β_b= 1.0 for plastic and compact sections

$= \frac{Z_e}{Z_p}$ for semi-compact sections.

Z_p, Z_e=plastic, and elastic section moduli of the cross-section, respectively.

- High shear case $V > 0.6V_d$

In such cases,

$$M_d = M_{dv} \tag{2.3}$$

where M_{dv} is designed for bending strength under high shear.

This reduced value is recommended to account for the effect of higher shear on the bending strength of the sections. M_{dv} is to be calculated as given in Clause 9.2.2 of IS 800-2007:

- Plastic or compact section:

$$M_{dv} = M_d - \beta_b(M_d - M_{fd}) \le 1.2\,\frac{Z_e f_y}{\gamma_{m0}} \qquad 2.4$$

Where $\beta = \left(\frac{2V}{V_d} - 1\right)^2$

M_d = Plastic design moment of the whole section.

V = Factored applied shear force.

V_d = Design shear strength.

M_{fd} = Plastic design strength of the cross-section area excluding the shear area, considering partial safety factor γ_{m0}.

- Semi-compact section

$$M_{dv} = \frac{Z_e f_y}{\gamma_{m0}} \qquad 2.5$$

2.5 SHEAR STRENGTH OF A LATERALLY SUPPORTED BEAM

The design shear strength of a section is given by Clause 8.4 of IS 800-2007:

$$V_d = \frac{A_v f_{yw}}{\sqrt{3}\,\gamma_{m0}} \qquad 2.6$$

Where A_v = shear area

f_{yw} = yield strength of the web.

The shear area may be calculated as given below:

- I and channel sections:

  (i) Major Axis bending:

  Hot-Rolled: $A_v = ht_w$

Welded: $A_v = dt_w$

(ii) Minor Axis bending:

Hot rolled or welded: $A_v = 2bt_f$

- Rectangular hollow sections of uniform thickness:
  (i) Loaded parallel to depth (h): $A_v = \frac{Ah}{b+h}$
  (ii) Loaded parallel to width (b): $A_v = \frac{Ab}{b+h}$
- Circular hollow tubes of uniform thickness: $A_v = \frac{2A}{\pi}$
- Plates and solid bars: $A_v = A$

where A = cross-section area
b = overall breadth of tubular section, breadth of I-section flanges
d = clear depth of web between flanges
h = overall depth of the section
t = thickness of the flange and

2.6 DEFLECTION LIMITS

The deflection should be computed using elastic theory under working load circumstances. The beam's maximum deflection should not exceed the limits in Table 6 of IS 800-2007.

Illustration 2.1: Design a laterally restrained beam that spans 5m, having a total factored load of 24 kN/m, including self-weight. The grade of steel used is Fe 415.

Solution:
Factored load (W)=24 kN/m,

f_y=250 N/mm, γ_{m0}= 1.1.

Factored maximum bending moment, $M = \frac{WL^2}{8} = \frac{24\times5^2}{8}$ = 75 kN-m.

But $M = \frac{f_y Z_e}{\gamma_{mo}}$

$Z_e = \frac{M_u \gamma_{mo}}{f_y} = \frac{75x10^6 \times 1.1}{250}$ = 330x10^3 mm^3.

Design shear force $= \frac{W_u l}{2} = \frac{24 \times 5}{2} = 60$ kN.

Let us try ISMB 250 @365.91 N/m. The properties are mentioned in Table I, Section A of SP: 6(1)-1964.

Table 2.1: Rolled steel beams (Section 1, SP: 6(1)-1964)

ISI HANDBOOK FOR STRUCTURAL ENGINEERS : STRUCTURAL STEEL SECTIONS

TABLE I ROLLED STEEL BEAMS

DIMENSIONS AND PROPERTIES

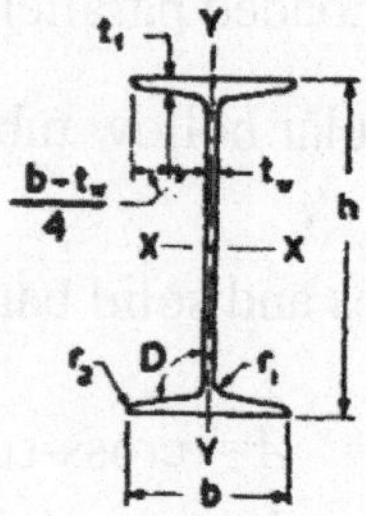

Designation	Weight per Metre w	Sectional Area a	Depth of Section h	Width of Flange b	Thickness of Flange t_f	Thickness of Web t_w	Moments of Inertia I_{xx}	I_{yy}	Radii of Gyration r_{xx}	r_{yy}
	kg	cm²	mm	mm	mm	mm	cm⁴	cm⁴	cm	cm
ISMB 250	37·3	47·55	250	125	12·5	6·9	5 131·6	334·5	10·39	2·65
ISMB 300	44·2	56·26	300	140	12·4	7·5	8 603·6	453·9	12·37	2·84
ISMB 350	52·4	66·71	350	140	14·2	8·1	13 630·3	537·7	14·29	2·84

Moduli of Section Z_{xx}	Z_{yy}	Radius at Root r_1	Radius at Toe r_2	Slope of Flange D	Connection Details h_1	h_2	b_1	C	g	g_1 (Min)	Maximum Size of Flange Rivet	Designation
cm³	cm³	mm	mm	degrees	mm	mm	mm	mm	mm	mm	mm	
410·5	53·5	13·0	6·5	98	194·1	27·95	59·05	4·95	65	65	22	ISMB 250
573·6	64·8	14·0	7·0	98	241·5	29·25	66·25	5·25	80	65	22	ISMB 300
778·9	76·8	14·0	7·0	98	288·0	31·00	65·95	5·55	80	65	22	ISMB 350

Width of flange (b)=125 mm,

Thickness of flange(t_f)=12.5 mm,

Thickness of web(t_w)= 6.9 mm,

Web depth (d_w) = h-2t_f=225 mm.

Root radius(r)=13 mm,

I_{xx} =5131.6 x10^4 mm^4,

Z_e=410.5 x10^3 mm^3,

Plastic section modulus (Z_p)=465.71x10^3 mm^3,

- Section classification

$$\epsilon = \sqrt{\frac{250}{f_y}} = \sqrt{\frac{250}{250}} = 1$$

$$\text{Flange overhang } b = \frac{125}{2} = 62.5 \text{ mm}$$

$$\frac{b}{t_f} = \frac{62.5}{12.5} = 5 < 9.4\epsilon$$

$$\frac{d}{t_w} = \frac{225}{6.9} = 32.6 < 84\epsilon$$

Hence, the section is plastic.

- Check for shear strength

Design shear force = V = 60 kN

Design shear strength of section-

$$V_d = \frac{f_{yh}t_w}{\sqrt{3}\,mo} = \frac{250x250x6.9}{\sqrt{3x1.1}} = 226347 = 226.35\ kN > 60 \text{ kN}$$

Hence ok.

Check for high or low shear-

$$0.6V_d = 0.6 \times 226.35 = 135.8 \text{ kN} > 60 \text{ kN}$$

Hence, it is a case of low shear. (V<0.6Vd)

- Shear buckling check-

d/t_w= 28.8<67€. Hence, this check is not required.

- Check for design moment capacity-

For plastic section β_b=1

So, design moment= $\frac{\beta b Z p f y}{\gamma m o} \leq \frac{1.2 Z e f y}{\gamma m o}$

$$= \frac{1x465.71x10^{3x250}}{1.1} \leq \frac{1.2x410.5x10^{3x250}}{1.1}$$

$$= 105.84\ \text{kN} - \text{m} \leq 111.954545\ \text{kN} - \text{m}$$

- Check for deflection

Working load(w)=24/1.5=16 kN/m=16 N/mm

Maximum deflection= $(5\ Wl^4)/384\ EI$ = $(5 \times 16 \times 5000^4)/(384 \times 2 \times 10^5 \times 5131.6 \times 10^4)$ mm = 12.68 mm

Permissible deflection= Span/300= 5000/300= 16.66 mm.

Hence, maximum deflection (12.68 mm) < Maximum permissible deflection (16.66 mm)

So ok.

SUMMARY

The steel beam design adheres to IS 800-2007 recommendations, aiming to safely carry bending, shear, and axial forces while maintaining strength, stability, and serviceability. The design considers material properties, load types, beam configuration, and support conditions. Key aspects include conforming to specified steel grades, considering load considerations, determining bending and shear strength, and satisfying deflection criteria. Section classification is crucial for beam stability under bending and shear stresses. Buckling and lateral stability are also important considerations, with the critical buckling moment calculated and resistance checked. Web shear and plate buckling are considered for deep beams with large shear forces. Safety factors ensure structural reliability and safety under varying load conditions.

EXERCISE

Make a few groups of students, each having five students. The students take on different roles, as mentioned below, and simulate interactions between stakeholders to finalise the beam design:

- Architect: Ensure the beam dimensions align with architectural aesthetics and space constraints.
- Construction Manager: Address practical challenges, such as beam transportation, erection, and on-site fabrication.
- Regulatory Agency: Confirm compliance with IS 800-2007 standards and local building codes.
- Client: Discuss cost implications and modifications to ensure the project stays within budget.

MULTIPLE CHOICE QUESTIONS

1. Consider the following statements:
   Lateral support in the case of a steel beam can be achieved by
   (1) Embedding its compression flange in a reinforced brick slab
   (2) Bracing the compression flanges of adjacent beams
   (3) Providing shear connectors on the compression flange
   Out of the above statements,
   A) 1, 2, and 3 are correct
   B) 2 and 3 are correct
   C) only 2 is correct
   D) only 1 is correct
2. As per IS specifications, the beam sections should be
   A) At least symmetrical about one of the principal axes
   B) Preferably plastic or compact sections only
   C) Rolled to furnish maximum sectional modulus
   D) All the above
3. Beams should be designed and checked for
   A) Flexural strength
   B) Stiffness
   C) Local buckling
   D) All the above

4. The effective length of the compression flange of a supported beam not restrained against torsion at ends is *K* times the span, where *K* is
   A) 0.70
   B) 1.00
   C) 0.85
   D) 1.20
5. In a simply supported beam of span *L*, each end is restrained against torsion, with the compression flange being unrestrained. According to IS 800-2007, the effective length of the compression flange will be equal to
   A) *L*
   B) 0.75 *L*
   C) 0.85 *L*
   D) 1.20 *L*
6. The design of a beam is governed by shear
   A) When the depth of the beam section is small, and the beam is loaded uniformly
   B) When large concentrated loads are placed near beam supports
   C) Both (a) and (b)
   D) None of the above is correct
7. Web crippling in steel beams occurs due to
   A) Column action of compression flange
   B) Failure of the web under concentrated load
   C) Excessive bending moment
   D) Secondary bending moment
8. Deflection limitations over beams are imposed because excessive deflection
   A) May create problems for roof drainage
   B) May cause undesirable twisting and distortion of end connections
   C) May cause psychological problems for the users
   D) All the above
9. The deflection of steel beams in buildings other than industrial buildings is limited to a span divided by
   A) 180
   B) 250
   C) 300
   D) 325
10. The lateral restraint at the supports for a laterally supported beam may be in the form of
   A) Web cleats

B) Partial depth end plates
C) Continuity with the adjacent span
D) Any of the above

11. Pick out the incorrect statement:
A) An I-section lintel in a masonry wall is designed as a laterally unsupported beam
B) Purlins are subjected to unsymmetrical bending
C) Purlins are designed as a continuous beam
D) The CG of purlins should coincide with the node points of the truss. The deflection of steel beams in buildings other than industrial buildings is limited to a span divided by

12. As per IS 800-2007, purlins are designed as
A) Simply supported beams
B) Cantilever beams
C) Continuous beams
D) Compression member

13. Sag roads are designed as
A) Compression members
B) Tension members
C) Laterally supported beams
D) Laterally unsupported beams

14. In a steel beam section, the web carries
A) The compression
B) The tension
C) The moment
D) The shear

15. To calculate the area of cover plates of a built-up beam, an allowance for rivet holes to be added
A) 10%
B) 13%
C) 18%
D) 15%

16. The steel beam of light section plain cement concrete is called
A) Filler joists
B) Concrete joists
C) Simple joists
D) Joists

17. The problem of lateral buckling can arise only in those steel beams that have
    A) Moment of inertia about the bending axis larger than the other
    B) Moment of inertia about the bending axis smaller than the other
    C) Fully supported compression flange
    D) None of the these
18. For a cantilever beam of length L, continuous at the support and unrestrained against torsion at the support and the end, the effective length (l) is equal to
    A) $l = L$
    B) $l = 2L$
    C) $l = 0.5L$
    D) $l = 3L$

ANSWERS TO MULTIPLE CHOICE QUESTIONS

1	2	3	4	5	6	7	8	9
B	A	D	D	A	C	B	D	C
10	**11**	**12**	**13**	**14**	**15**	**16**	**17**	**18**
D	D	C	B	D	B	A	B	D

SHORT ANSWER TYPE QUESTIONS

1. What is the primary function of a beam in a steel structure?
2. What are the common types of steel beams used in construction?
3. What is the difference between supported and cantilever beams?
4. What is the role of shear force and bending moment in the design of a steel beam?
5. What is lateral-torsional buckling, and how can it affect steel beams?
6. What factors affect the moment capacity of a steel beam?
7. How is the section modulus of a steel beam related to its strength?
8. What is the difference between elastic and plastic section modulus?
9. What is a web stiffener, and when is it required in beam design?
10. Explain the significance of the moment of inertia in the design of a steel beam.
11. What are the advantages of using I-beams over other beam sections in steel structures?
12. What are the typical design considerations for steel beams subjected to concentrated loads?
13. How do we prevent deflection in long-span steel beams?
14. What is a composite beam, and how does it differ from a regular steel beam?
15. What are India's principal design codes or standards for steel beam design?

16. Why are rolled I-sections widely used as beam members?
17. What are the checks to be performed for beam member design?
18. What are castellated sections, and under what conditions are they used?
19. What is the difference between the bending and buckling of a beam member?
20. What is meant by lateral torsional buckling of a beam member?
21. Under what conditions can lateral buckling occur?
22. Under what conditions can a beam member be assumed laterally restrained?
23. What is the difference between column buckling and beam buckling?
24. An I-beam loaded perpendicular to the minor axis does not buckle. Why?
25. What is the local buckling of a beam member?
26. Differentiate between local and lateral buckling of beams.

LONG ANSWER TYPE QUESTIONS

1. Explain the concept of elastic and plastic behaviour of steel in the context of beam design. How does the design approach differ when considering elastic vs. plastic analysis for steel beams?
2. What is the moment of inertia, and why is it essential to design steel beams? How does it affect the load-carrying capacity of the beam?
3. Differentiate between simply supported, fixed, and continuous beams regarding moment distribution and structural behaviour.
4. How do shear forces and bending moments influence the design of steel beams? Explain with the help of shear force and bending moment diagrams.
5. Discuss the concept of flexural strength in steel beams. How do you determine the maximum bending stress in a beam subjected to various types of loading?
6. Explain the procedure to design a beam for pure bending and bending with shear. How do these conditions affect the selection of beam size and shape?
7. Describe the phenomenon of web buckling in steel beams. What are the key factors influencing the likelihood of web buckling, and how can it be prevented in design?
8. What is shear capacity in steel beams, and how is it calculated? Discuss the importance of web thickness in resisting shear forces in beams.
9. Explain the criteria for selecting standard steel sections (e.g., I-sections, H-sections, box sections) for beam design. How does the choice of section influence the overall strength and economy of the design?
10. Compare rolled and fabricated steel sections in steel beam design. What factors should be considered when deciding between these two options?

11. What is lateral-torsional buckling in steel beams? Explain the factors that influence lateral-torsional buckling and the design strategies to prevent it.
12. How does unbraced length affect the lateral-torsional buckling strength of a steel beam? Discuss the impact of providing lateral support along the length of the beam.
13. Discuss the significance of serviceability limit states in the design of steel beams. How do deflection limits influence the overall design, and what methods can be used to control deflections?
14. What role do vibration criteria play in the serviceability design of steel beams, especially in structures like bridges or long-span floors
15. Explain the role of connections (welded or bolted) in steel beam design. What are the key considerations in designing beam-to-column and beam-to-beam connections in steel structures?
16. How do end connections influence steel beams' overall moment and shear capacity? Discuss the role of moment-resisting connections in steel frames.
17. What is a composite steel beam, and how does it differ from a non-composite beam? Explain the benefits and design considerations of using composite beams in building construction.
18. Explain the design considerations for curved steel beams. What additional factors must be considered compared to straight beams?
19. How are castellated beams designed, and what are their advantages and limitations? Discuss how the creation of web openings affects the strength and stability of the beam.
20. Design a supported steel beam of span $L = 5$ m, carrying a uniformly distributed load w=15 kN/m. Use steel with f_y=250 MPa.

TUTORIAL

An industrial floor requires steel beams to carry machinery loads. Each beam spans 6 m and must support a point load of 50 kN from heavy equipment at mid-span, in addition to a uniformly distributed load of 10 kN/m.

- Calculate the maximum bending moment and shear force due to the point load and UDL.
- Select a beam section and verify its bending and shear capacity.
- Check for deflection limits to ensure floor serviceability.
- Discuss the impact of concentrated loads on the web and propose web stiffening measures if required.

KNOW MORE

For more information related to this topic, scan the QR code.

OR

Type this link in your browser

https://www.steel-insdag.org/assets/frontend/trmpdf/Chapter9.pdf

BIBLIOGRAPHY

1. Arya, A. S. (2014). *Structural Design in Steel*, Nem Chand & Bros, Roorkee.
2. Bureau of Indian Standards. (2007). IS 800-2007, *General Construction in Steel – Code of Practice*, New Delhi.
3. Duggal, S. K. (2017). *Limit State Design of Steel Structures*, Tata McGraw-Hill Publishing Company: New Delhi.
4. Sairam, K.S., Design of Steel Structures, Pearson Publication, Chennai, Delhi.
5. Shah, V. L., and Gore, V. (2019). *Limit State Design of Steel Structures*, Structures Publications, Pune.
6. Subramanian, N. (2017). *Design of Steel Structures limit state method*, Oxford University Press.

3 DESIGN OF REINFORCED CONCRETE BEAMS BY LIMIT STATE METHOD

UNIT SPECIFICS

In this unit, students will be introduced to the Limit State Design approach as per IS 456, which ensures that reinforced concrete structures are designed to remain safe and functional throughout their service life. The unit covers the stress block diagram, which helps understand the stress distribution in a concrete beam under loading. It also introduces the design of singly and doubly reinforced sections, explaining the concepts of under-reinforced, over-reinforced, and balanced sections. Students will learn to design singly reinforced beams, calculate the ultimate moment of resistance, and solve numerical problems. The design of doubly reinforced beams will also be explored, focusing on the stress and strain diagrams, the calculation of neutral axis depth, and the determination of tension and compression reinforcement areas. Through practical examples and numerical problems, students will develop the ability to design and analyse reinforced concrete beams effectively.

RATIONALE

The rationale for this unit is to provide students with a solid foundation in reinforced concrete design, focusing on the Limit State Design approach as outlined in IS 456-2000. This unit introduces essential concepts such as stress block diagrams and the design of both singly and doubly reinforced beams. Through practical application, including calculating the ultimate moment of resistance and designing beam sections, students will learn to accurately determine reinforcement areas and design safe, efficient structural elements. By solving numerical problems, students will develop a deeper understanding of concrete behaviour under load and the design of reinforced concrete sections, preparing them for real-world engineering challenges.

PRE-REQUISITE

Basic mathematics

UNIT OUTCOMES

The list of outcomes of this unit is as follows:

U3-O1: Understand Limit State Method

U3-O2: Design of singly reinforced beam

U3-O3: Design of doubly reinforced beam

U3-O4: Understanding stress-strain diagram

Unit Outcomes	Expected Mapping with Course Outcomes (1- Weak correlation; 2- Medium correlation; 3- Strong correlation)				
	CO-1	CO-2	CO-3	CO-4	CO-5
U3-O1	2	3	2	-	2
U3-O2	-	3	2	-	3
U3-O3	-	3	2	-	3
U3-O4	3	-	3	-	1

3.1 INTRODUCTION

Reinforced Concrete Structure has replaced conventional building materials like stone, timber, and steel. Any reinforced concrete structure assembles basic structural elements like beams, columns, footings, slabs, and walls. Therefore, the design of reinforced concrete structures lies in the design of these basic structural elements, i.e., beams, columns, slabs, and walls. The design aims to ensure that structures can withstand the loads and forces they will encounter during their lifetime.

The challenge in structural engineering is to balance safety, functionality, and economy in designing various components like beams, columns, and slabs. Key objectives in design include resisting loads, limiting deflections, and preventing failure. This chapter highlights the shift from older methods (like the Working Stress Method) to more modern approaches, such as the Limit State Method (LSM), which offers a more accurate, flexible, and economical way to design structures.

3.1.1 Design Consideration

The goal of structural design is to create a structure that performs its intended function throughout its lifespan while ensuring adequate safety (strength, stability, and structural integrity), serviceability (stiffness and durability), and cost-effectiveness (economy) at service or working loads. The meaning of safety, serviceability, and cost-effectiveness concerning the design of a structure is given below:

Safety

It ensures the structure remains stable, strong, and intact, with a low probability of failure. This includes maintaining structural integrity under normal loads, extreme earthquakes, or strong winds. Collapse may result from various causes, such as exceeding load-bearing capacity, overturning, sliding, buckling, fatigue, or fracture. In addition, safety considerations also ensure structural integrity by minimising the risk of progressive collapse.

Serviceability

It refers to the structure's ability to function satisfactorily under normal load conditions without causing discomfort to users due to excessive deflections, cracking, and vibrations. Other factors like durability and insulation (acoustic and thermal) are also important considerations under serviceability. It's important to note that a design that meets safety requirements may not necessarily ensure serviceability. For example, while a thin reinforced concrete slab may be strong enough to avoid collapse, the occupants of the building could still suffer from problems like low sound and thermal insulation.

Cost-effectiveness

Balancing safety and serviceability often require increased design margins, which increases the structure's cost. Therefore, when considering the overall economy, the additional cost of enhancing safety must be weighed against the potential risks and damages arising from structural failure or serviceability issues.

3.1.2 Design Philosophies

Over time, numerous design philosophies have emerged globally for the design of reinforced concrete structures. Every design philosophy is based on fundamental assumptions and reflects a particular approach. The earliest is the Working Stress Method (WSM), grounded in linear elastic theory, which is still used in some countries, though it has been replaced mainly by the modern Limit States Method (LSM). The limitation of WSM is that it fails to give relative importance to different loads that act on the structure, i.e., live load, dead load, snow, and seismic load. In the latest version of IS 456-2000, the provisions of WSM of design have been shifted from the main text to the code of Annexure 'B' to emphasise LSM.

The Ultimate Load Method (ULM) of design relies on the strength of concrete ultimate loads, developed in the 1950s, focuses on reinforced concrete's strength under maximum loads and gained acceptance as an alternative to WSM. ULM was introduced in the ACI and British codes in the late 1950s and the Indian Code in 1964. It was later recognised that accurately estimating loads and material properties involves significant uncertainty. Designing a structure to handle the worst possible loads makes it very safe, but it probably won't experience those extreme loads. This method can raise costs and make the structure uneconomical. However, probabilistic design concepts, which depend on the theory of probability to quantify design risk using failure probability, began in the mid-1960s. The risk associated with the design of structures was quantified in terms of the likelihood of structure failure.

Although theoretically sound, these methods were considered too complex for widespread professional use. To simplify them, many (partial) safety factors were introduced, leading to the development of the reliability-based Limit States Method (LSM), first adopted by the European Committee for Concrete (CEB) and the International Federation of Prestressing (FIP). Later, the limit state design method was adopted in the Indian Code (IS 456-1978.)

3.2 LIMIT STATE DESIGN

3.2.1 Principle of Limit State

The principle of limit state design rests on both ultimate limit states and serviceability limit states.

Ultimate limit states (ULS)
These states relate to conditions beyond which the structure would no longer be safe. These include collapse due to material failure, buckling, or yielding of steel reinforcement in concrete.

Serviceability limit states (SLS)
These relate to the conditions that affect the structure's usability without causing users discomfort. For example, excessive deflection, cracking, or vibration is considered in SLS. The structure should be designed to remain functional throughout its intended lifespan without needing major repairs.

The Limit State Design approach ensures a structure can be safe and serviceable under different loading conditions. This dual approach provides a comprehensive understanding of how a structure will behave under varying circumstances, ensuring safety while optimising material usage.

3.2.2 Concept of Limit State

The Limit State Method (LSM) is a major advancement in structural design above conventional methods. LSM adopts a more thorough approach by considering both safety and serviceability, in contrast to the Working Stress Method (WSM), which only takes service load conditions into account, and the Ultimate Load Method (ULM), which only takes ultimate load conditions into account. LSM is based on a statistical concept of safety and the associated statistical probability of failure. The limit State Method revolves around the idea of 'limit states,' which mark the boundary between acceptable performance and failure. A Limit State is the state of 'about to collapse' or 'impending failure', beyond which the structure is no longer useful, meaning it either collapses or is no longer serviceable. In LSM, two main types of limit states are defined as follows:

Limit State

Limit State of Collapse | *Limit State of Serviceability*

Limit state of collapse (Ultimate limit state)

This limit state deals with the strength of the structure in terms of collapse, overturning, sliding, buckling, fatigue, and fracture.

Various limit states of collapses are:

Limit state of serviceability

This limit state deals with the deformation of the structure to the point where it becomes unfit for use due to excessive deflection, cracking, vibrations, leakage, and similar issues. Limit state of serviceability can be attributed to:

- Deflection
- Excessive vibrations
- Corrosion
- Cracking (excluding the tensile strength of concrete)

A key feature of LSM is its use of multiple safety factors to address different types of failure, ensuring structural integrity and functionality. By providing a more balanced and rational approach, LSM ensures that a structure can withstand its maximum load capacity without collapsing and guarantees that it remains functional and comfortable under normal use. This way, LSM represents a modern design philosophy that integrates safety, performance, and reliability, setting it apart from older design methods.

3.3 IS 456-2000 RECOMMENDATION FOR DESIGNING STRUCTURES USING LSM

3.3.1 Characteristic Load and Strength

The characteristic load and strength are statistical concepts used in the design process. They help ensure that structures are designed conservatively enough to handle unforeseen extreme conditions without being overdesigned.

Characteristic load

Defined as the load that *"has a 95 percent probability of not being exceeded during the structure's life"* (Cl. 36.2, IS 456-2000). However, without statistical data on loads, the nominal values for dead, live, and wind loads should be taken from IS 875 (Parts 1-3)-1987, while the values for seismic (earthquake) loads should be sourced from IS 1893: 2002. The characteristic load ensures that the design is based on realistic assumptions about loading conditions while using partial safety factors, which increases confidence that the structure will remain safe even under extreme circumstances. For the sake of simplicity, it may be assumed that the variation of these loads and strength follow normal distribution laws as shown in Fig.3.1 Normal distribution means distribution symmetric about mean values.

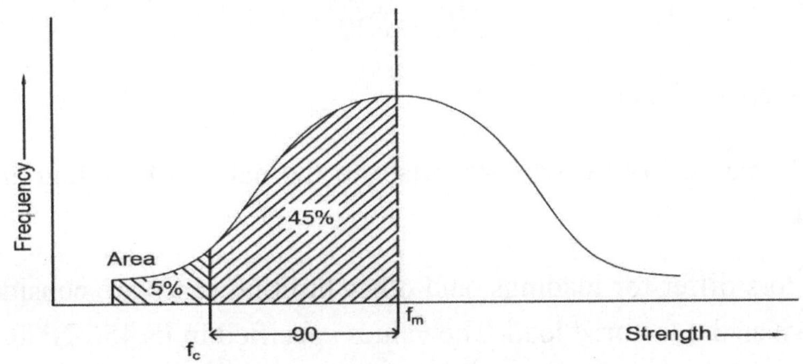

Figure 3.1: Characteristic load

Characteristic strength

The strength that one can safely assume for the material (concrete and steel) is termed characteristic strength. It is obtained by dividing the characteristic compressive strength of the cube by a factor of 1.5 to account for variations in loading conditions (other than uniaxial compression) and variations in the shape of the concrete (other than a cube of 150 mm). This is based on the statistical analysis of the test below, in which not more than 5% of the results are expected to fail. In this case, the normal distribution is also assumed, as shown in Fig. 3.2 The characteristic strength of a material is the value below which not more than 5% of the test results fall. It represents the material's capability to withstand forces. For example, concrete's characteristic compressive strength is defined for 28 days. These characteristic values are used along with partial safety factors to ensure that the structure is designed to be strong and reliable.

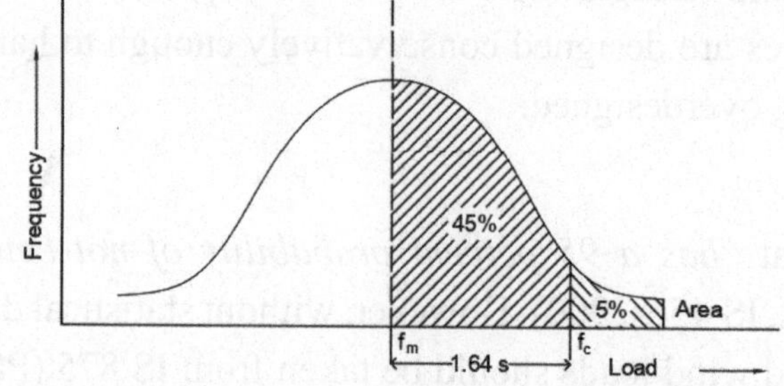

Figure 3.2: Characteristic strength

3.3.2 Partial Safety Factor of Loads

The design loads for various limit states are obtained as the product of the characteristic loads and partial safety factor and are expressed as:

$$F_d = F.\gamma_f$$

where F = Characteristic Load

γ_f = Load Partial safety factor appropriate to the nature of loading and the limit state being considered.

Partial safety factors differ for loadings, and other limiting cases are considered. The design load is also known as the factored load. The values specified in IS 456-2000 are mentioned in Table 3.1.

Table 3.1: Values of partial safety factor γ_f for loads (Table 18 of IS 456-2000)

SI. No.	Load Combination	Limit State of Collapse			Limit State of Serviceability		
		DL	IL	WL	DL	IL	WL
1	DL + IL	1.5	1.5	-	1.0	1.0	-
2	DL + WL						
	Case						
	(i) DL contributing to Stability	0.9	-	1.5	1.0	-	1.0
	(ii) DL assisting overturning	1.5	-	1.5	1.0	-	1.0
3	DL + IL + WL	1.2	1.2	1.2	1.0	0.8	0.8

Notes:

- While considering earthquake effects, substitute Earthquake Load (EL) for Wind Load (WL).
- For serviceability limit states, the value provided in Table 3.1 applies to short-term effects. When evaluating long-term effects due to creep, only the Dead Load (DL) and the portion of the Live Load (LL) expected to be permanent should be considered.

3.3.3 Partial Safety Factor of Materials

The design strength of the material f_d is given by,

$$f_d = f / \gamma_m$$

Where f = characteristic strength of the material

γ_m = partial safety factor appropriate to the material and the considered limit state

f_d = design strength of the material

The partial factor of safety is different from different materials and limit states. The values recommended by the IS 456-2000 are shown in Table 3.2.

Table 3.2: Partial factor of safety for material strength (Clause 36.4.2 of IS 456-2000)

Material	Limit State	
	Collapse	Deflection
Concrete	1.5	1.0
Steel	1.15	1.0

3.4 DESIGN OF SINGLY REINFORCED SECTION

3.4.1 Introduction to Singly Reinforced Beam

In structural engineering, beams are essential components in various constructions. The singly reinforced beam is vital in reinforced concrete design. It is reinforced on one side at the tension zone with steel bars to improve strength.

Concrete is strong in compression yet weak in tension. Steel reinforcement is added in the tension zone where tensile stresses arise to address this weakness. In singly reinforced beams, steel bars are positioned in the lower half, where tensile forces peak, while the upper compression zone relies on the concrete's compressive strength.

This design provides an economical option for structural requirements. Singly reinforced beams are prevalent in residential and commercial buildings, where moderate loads and cost-effectiveness are crucial. The synergy between concrete's compressive strength and steel's tensile capacity renders these beams suitable for standard construction applications.

Nevertheless, limitations exist. Singly reinforced beams may be inadequate for heavy loads or long spans, necessitating doubly reinforced beams or advanced designs for safety. Still, singly reinforced beams' simplicity and economic viability are fundamental in reinforced concrete design, making their understanding vital for aspiring engineers.

3.4.2 Assumptions

As per Clause 38.1 of IS 456-2000, the following assumptions are made while analysing the reinforced concrete beam by LSM:

- Plane sections normal to the beam axis remain plane after bending. i.e., in an initially straight beam, strain varies linearly over the depth of the section. Thus, the strain diagram is linear, as shown in Fig.3.3.
- The maximum compressive strain in concrete at the outmost fibre (ε_u) is taken as 0.0035, regardless of whether the beam is under–reinforced (amount of tensile reinforcement provided is less than the balanced reinforcement) or over–reinforced (amount of tensile reinforcement exceeds the balanced reinforcement).
- The stress-strain curve for concrete has a parabolic shape up to 0.002 strain and then constant up to the limit state of 0.0035. However, IS 456-2000 does not prevent using

other shapes like rectangles and trapezoidal, which result in the prediction of strength in substantial agreement with the result of the tests.

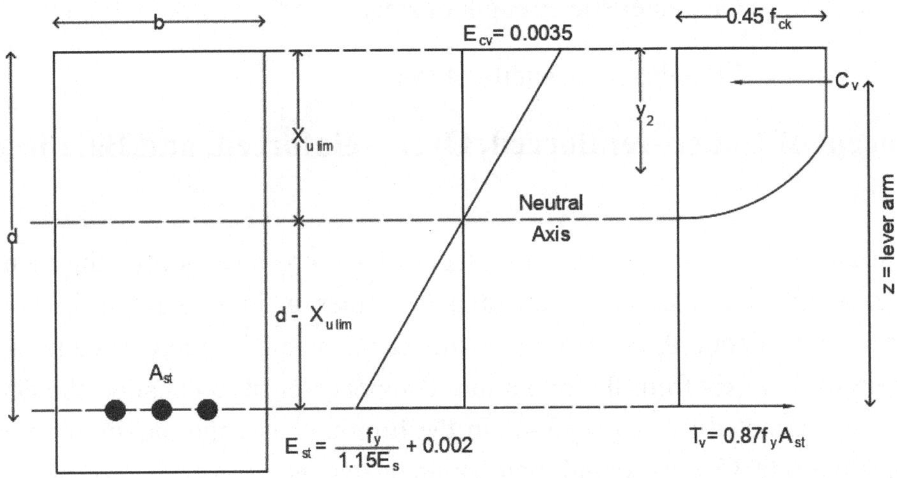

Figure 3.3: Reinforced concrete rectangular section at ultimate limit state of flexure singly reinforced beam

For design purposes, the compressive strength in the structure (size effect) may be assumed to be 0.67 times the characteristic strength. In addition to this, the partial safety factor γ_m may be taken as 1.5. This means the maximum compressive strength in the extreme fibre of the section will be 0.67 over 1.5 f_{ck} equals 0.446 f_{ck}, or it may be taken as $0.45 f_{ck}$ also.

- Tension is borne entirely by steel; hence, the tensile strength of concrete is ignored. Clause B-1.3 (b) of IS 456-2000 states that all tensile stresses must be taken up by reinforcement and none by concrete.
- For design purposes, the compressive strength of concrete may be assumed to be 0.67 times the characteristic strength of concrete. The partial safety factor of $\gamma_c = 1.5$ shall be applied in addition to this.
- For design purposes, the partial safety factor for steel is taken as $\gamma_s = 1.15$, i.e.

$$\text{Design stress of steel} = \frac{f_y}{1.15} = 0.87 f_y$$

- The maximum strain (ε_{st}) in the tension reinforcement at the level of the centroid of reinforcement steel at the ultimate limit state shall not be less than ε_{st}, which is defined as:

$$\varepsilon_{st} = \frac{0.87\, f_y}{E_s} + 0.002$$

where, f_y = Characteristic strength of steel

and E_s = Modulus of elasticity of steel

3.4.3 Concept of Under–reinforced, Over–reinforced, and Balanced Section

In bending, strain varies linearly across the depth of the cross-section of the member. One beam edge is in maximum compression, and the other is in maximum tension. Hence, somewhere across the depth, there is an axis with zero tension. The axis is called the neutral axis. The depth of this axis from the maximum compression fibre is called the depth of the neutral axis and is denoted by x_u (Fig.3.4). In the limiting case, the maximum compressive strain in concrete is 0.0035, corresponding to strain in steel is

$$\varepsilon_s = \left(\frac{d - x_u}{x_u}\right) 0.0035$$

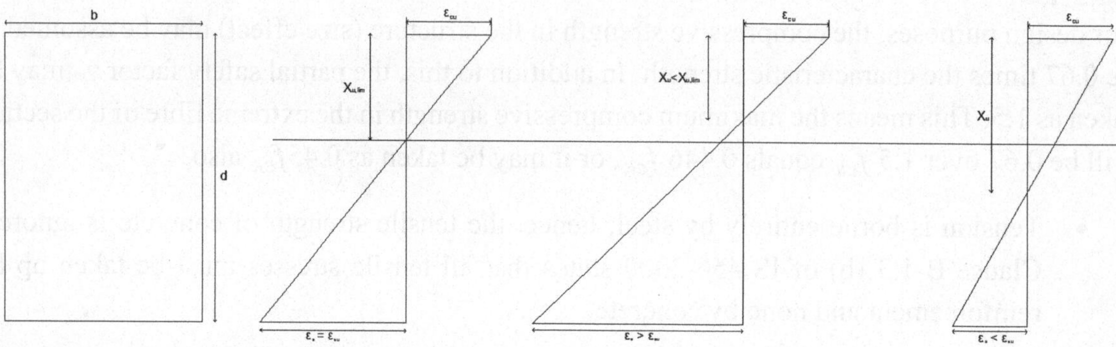

(a) Cross section (b) Balanced (c) Under Reinforced (d) Over Reinforced

Figure 3.4: Stress-strain curve of different sections

From the stress-strain curve (Fig.3.4), we find that when this value exceeds $\frac{0.87 f_y}{E_s} + 0.002$, the stress in steel is yield stress f_y.

A section is called a balanced section if the strain in concrete and steel reaches their limiting values simultaneously for the same applied moment. In other words, in balanced sections, maximum compressive strain ε_c in concrete reaches 0.0035 when the tensile strain in steel reaches its limiting value of

$$\varepsilon_{su} = \frac{0.87 f_y}{E_S} + 0.002$$

A section in which tensile strain reaches yield strain of $\frac{0.87 f_y}{E_S} + 0.002$ earlier to compressive strain in concrete reaching the limiting value of 0.0035, is called under–reinforced section. In these cases, the final steel reaches yield strain as the moment increases. The stress in steel remains the same (f_y), but the strain increases. When the moment corresponding to 0.0035 strain in concrete is reached, concrete is crushed, and failure occurs. The excess strain in steel beyond $\frac{0.87 f_y}{E_S} + 0.002$ amounts to considerable cracks in the concrete. The deflection will increase. They serve as a warning to the user and allow one to take precautions to avoid disaster. Hence, IS 456-2000 specifies that the maximum strain in tension reinforced shall not be less than $\frac{0.87 f_y}{E_S} + 0.002$. In other words, IS 456-2000 prefers design of under reinforced sections and at the most, it can be a balanced section. This type of failure in the under-reinforced section is called primary tensile failure.

R.C. sections in which the limiting strain in concrete is reached earlier than the yield strain of steel are called over-reinforced sections. At failure, steel is not yielded, and concrete bursts out. As there are no failure warnings in such sections, the IS 456-2000 recommends avoiding such design. Hence, a designer should not provide extra steel to create a feeling of safety. No doubt, providing extra steel increases the load-carrying capacity of the section, but in case of overloading, it results in sudden collapse.

If $x_{u\,lim}$ is the value of depth of the neutral axis in the balanced section, it may be noted than $x_{u\,lim}$ in under reinforced sections and $x_u > x_{u\,lim}$ in over reinforced sections, as shown in Fig.3.4.

The basic assumption here is that the plane section before bending remains the plane even after bending, leading to the linear strain variation along the cross-section.

Stress block parameter

The stress block diagram (Fig.3.3) is an essential structural design tool, especially reinforced concrete design. It helps visualise stress distribution across a cross-section of a structural element, like a beam or column, under load. The stress block represents the variation of compressive stresses in concrete and the tension in reinforcement.

The diagram illustrating the distribution of compressive stress in concrete along the depth x_u of the section is referred to as the stress block. Since the strain diagram is linear across this depth x_u, the shape of the stress block is the same as the idealised stress-strain curve of concrete. At the neutral axis, the stress is zero. It varies parabolically upto a height of 4/7 x_u i.e., (0.002/0.0035) x_u and has a constant value equal to the design stress of 0.446 f_{ck} i.e. $0.67 \times \frac{1}{1.5} f_{ck}$ for the $\frac{3}{7} x_u$ i.e., $\left[\frac{0.0035 - 0.002}{0.0035} x_u\right]$. The shape of stress block is as shown in Fig. 3.3.

The area of stress block may be found as explained below:

Area A of stress block = Area of rectangular portion + Area of parabolic portion

$$= 0.446 f_{ck} \times \frac{3}{7} x_u + \frac{2}{3} \times 0.446 f_{ck} \times \frac{4}{7} x_u$$

$$= 0.361 f_{ck} x_u$$

$$= 0.36 f_{ck} x_u \text{ (As recommended by IS 456-2000 code)}$$

Now we look at $0.36 f_{ck}$ as the average stress over the depth x_u (Clause 3.1)

Area of stress block = $f_{av} x_u$

Then, compressive force on the section,

$$C = b x_u f_{av}$$

$$= b x_u 0.36 f_{ck}$$

$$= k_1 f_{ck} b x_u$$

= 0.36 and is defined as a stress block parameter.

Distance of the centre of compressive force from the extreme compression fibre

By taking moments around the extreme compression edge (top edge), we get

$$C\bar{x} = C_1 x_1 + C_2 x_2$$

Where C = Total compressive force on the section

$\bar{x}$ = Distance of centre of gravity from compression edge

C_1 = Compressive force corresponding to a rectangular portion of the stress block

x_1 = Distance of centroid of C_1 from top fibre

C_2 = Compressive force corresponding to a parabolic portion of the stress block

x_2 = Distance of centroid of C_2

Now, $C = 0.36\, f_{ck} b x_u$

$$A_1 = 0.446\, f_{ck} b \frac{3}{7} x_u$$

$$x_1 = \frac{1}{2} \times \frac{3}{7} x_u = \frac{3}{14} x_u$$

$$A_2 = \frac{2}{3} \times 0.446 f_{ck} \times b \times \frac{4}{7} x_u$$

$$x_u = \frac{3}{7} x_u + \frac{3}{8}\left(\frac{4}{7} x_u\right),$$

Since the distance of the parabola of depth $'a'$ from wider ends is $\frac{3}{8}\ a$

$$= \frac{3}{7}(1 + 0.5) x_u = \frac{4.5}{7} x_u$$

Hence, we get

$$0.36 f_{ck} b x_u \bar{x} = 0.446 f_{ck} \times b \frac{3}{7} x_u \times \frac{3}{14} x_u + \frac{2}{3} \times 0.446 f_{ck} \times b \frac{4}{7} x_u \times \frac{4.5}{7} x_u$$

$$\bar{x} = 0.417 x_u \approx 0.42 x_u \text{ (As per IS 456-2000)}$$

$$= k_2 x_u$$

Where k_2= 0.42 is another important parameter of the stress block parameter.

3.4.4 Depth of Neutral Axis

Beams are assumed to fail in bending when the strain in concrete reaches the limiting compression strain of $\varepsilon_{cu} = 0.0035$. But in all cases of design tensile strain in steel need not be equal to limiting strain $\varepsilon_{su} = 0.002 + \frac{0.87\, f_y}{E_s}$. It can be less or more than it. However, designs with $\varepsilon < \varepsilon_{su}$ (over-reinforced sections) are to be avoided. Hence, in all cases:

Total compression $C = 0.36 f_{ck} b x_u$

And total tension $T = f_s A_{st}$

Where f_s is the stress in steel corresponding to the strain of 0.0035 in concrete [note, maximum design values of $f_s = 0.87f_y$]

Equilibrium requirement in horizontal direction fives (Fig.3.3) $C = T$

$$0.36\, f_{ck} b x_u = f_s A_{st}$$

or,
$$\frac{x_u}{d} = \frac{f_s A_{st}}{0.36 f_{ck} bd}$$

Limiting depth of the neutral axis

From the strain diagram (Fig.3.3) (NA for balanced section)

$$\frac{\varepsilon_s}{d - x_u} = \frac{0.0035}{x_u}$$

$$\frac{x_u}{d - x_u} = \frac{0.0035}{\varepsilon_s}$$

$$\frac{x_u}{d} = \frac{0.0035}{\varepsilon_s + 0.0035}$$

To avoid compression failure, IS 456-2000 recommends minimum strain corresponding 0.0035 strain in steel as

$$\varepsilon_{s\,min} = 0.87\frac{f_y}{E_s} + 0.002$$

The limiting value of x_u is given by the expression

$$\frac{x_{u\,lim}}{d} = \frac{0.0035}{0.87\frac{f_y}{E_s} + 0.002 + 0.0035} = \frac{0.0035}{0.87\frac{f_y}{E_s} + 0.0055}$$

Since $E = 2 \times 10^5$ N/mm^2 for all types of steels,

$\frac{x_{u\,lim}}{d}$ values for various types of steels are shown in Table 3.3.

Table 3.3: Limiting values of depth of neutral axis

Types of steel	f_y **(N/mm^2)**	$\frac{x_{u\,lim}}{d}$
Mild Steel (Fe 250)	250	0.53
Fe 415	415	0.48
Fe 500	500	0.46

Depth of neutral axis for under-reinforced sections

For under-reinforced sections, strain in steel is greater than its limiting value. Hence, from the idealised stress-strain curve, we get $f_s = 0.87f_y$; substituting it in the equation, we get,

$$\frac{x_u}{d} = \frac{0.87f_yA_{st}}{0.36f_{ck}bd}$$

Depth of neutral axis for over-reinforced sections

For over-reinforced sections, $\varepsilon_s < \varepsilon_{s\,lim}$. Hence the actual strain in steel at failure ε_s is to be found. Then, using a stress-strain diagram for steel, the corresponding stress is to be found. Since ε_s and x_u are interdependent, it is not possible to get one value from the other. A trial and error method is to be used. However, a designer has to note that such sections are not to be designed. If such sections already exist, we need this procedure to find the depth of the neutral axis.

Strength of rectangular section in flexure

The flexure strength of the R.C. section is also known as the moment carrying capacity of the section. The compressive force C in concrete and tensile force T in steel are equal and opposite and are separated by distance $d - 0.42x_u$ (Fig.3.3), called lever arm (LA). Hence, they form a couple. The couple moment is the moment of resistance, and it is called moment carrying capacity when $\varepsilon_c = 0.0035$.

Thus, moment carrying capacity is given by:

$$M_u = C.\ \text{Lever Arm}$$

$$= 0.36\ f_{ck}bx_u(d - 0.42x_u)$$

$$= 0.36\ f_{ck}\frac{x_u}{d}\left(1 - 0.42\frac{x_u}{d}\right)bd^2$$

M_u may be called the strength of the section in flexure. For the limiting case of a balanced section:

$$M_{u\,lim} = 0.36\ f_{ck}\frac{x_{u\,lim}}{d}\ (1 - 0.42\ \frac{x_{u\,lim}}{d})bd^2$$

$$= kf_{ck}bd^2$$

Where $k = 0.36\ f_{ck}\frac{x_{u\,lim}}{d}\left(1 - 0.42\frac{x_{u\,lim}}{d}\right)$. Substituting the values of $\frac{x_{u\,lim}}{d}$ for different steel grades (Table 3.3), we get the values of k for finding $M_{u\,lim}$ for various steel grades, as shown in Table 3.4.

Table 3.4: Limiting depth of neutral axis for balanced section

Type of steel	$\frac{x_{u\,lim}}{d}$	$M_{u\,lim}$
Fe 250 (Mild Steel)	0.53	$0.148 f_{ck} b d^2$
Fe 415	0.48	$0.138 f_{ck} b d^2$
Fe 500	0.46	$0.133 f_{ck} b d^2$

Illustration 3.1: Find the neutral axis's limiting value, steel area, and moment of resistance so that the section is balanced. The steel grade is Fe 415, and the grade of concrete is M25. The Overall depth of the section is 700 mm, and the width of the section is 300 mm. Take effective cover as 40 mm.

Solution:

Limiting value of neutral axis = $0.48d = 0.48 \times (700 - 40) = 316.8$ mm

Limiting area of steel= $A_{st} = 0.00048 f_{ck} bd = 0.00048 \times 25 \times 300 \times 660$

$= 2376 \text{ mm}^2$

Limiting percentage of tensile steel = $0.048 f_{ck}$

$= 0.048 \times 25 = 1.2\%$

Limiting moment of resistance = $0.138\, f_{ck}\, b\, d^2$

$= 0.138 \times 25 \times 300 \times 660^2$

$= 450.846 \times 10^6$ N-mm

$= 450.846$ kN-m.

Illustration 3.2: Find the neutral axis depth (Limiting) if the grade of steel used is Fe 550 and the concrete grade used is M25. Consider the effective depth of the section as 570 mm.

Solution:

Limiting value of neutral axis = $\left[\frac{700}{1100+0.87 f_y}\right] d$

$= \left[\frac{700}{1100+(0.87 \times 550)}\right] \times 570$

$= 252.7716$ mm.

Illustration 3.3: Find the depth of the limiting neutral axis for a rectangular reinforced concrete beam of section (300 mm x 500 mm) with a clear cover of 20 mm. The diameter of the reinforced bar is 20 mm, and the grade of steel used is Fe 500.

Solution:

For Fe 500, the maximum depth of the neutral axis = $0.46d$

$$= 0.46 \times (500 - \varphi/2 - \text{clear cover})$$

$$= 0.46 \times (500 - 10 - 20) \text{ mm}$$

$$= 216.2 \text{ mm.}$$

3.4.5 Approximate Expression for Moment of Resistance

In the case of the under-reinforced or balanced section, where x_u is for under reinforced or balanced section, where $x_u \leq x_{u\,lim}$, the stress in steel reaches the limiting value of $0.87f_y$ earlier. Hence, the equilibrium equation for horizontal forces gives,

$$C = T$$

$$0.36\, f_{ck} b x_u = 0.87\, f_y Ast$$

$$x_u = \frac{0.87 f_y Ast}{0.36 f_{ck} b}$$

The moment equilibrium equation gives,

$$M_u = T \times LA = 0.87\, f_y Ast\,(d - 0.42 x_u)$$

$$= 0.87\, f_y Ast\,[d - 0.42 \times \frac{0.87 f_y Ast}{0.36 f_{ck} b}]$$

$$= 0.87 f_y Ast\, d[1 - 1.015 \times \frac{Ast}{bd}\frac{f_y}{f_{ck}}]$$

IS 456 – 2000, permits the approximation of the above expression as

$$M_u = 0.87\, f_y Ast\, d[1 - \frac{Ast}{bd}\frac{f_y}{f_{ck}}]$$

In case of over-reinforced sections ($x_u \geq x_{u\,lim}$), the actual moment of resistance of the section may be obtained by usual formula $C \times LA$ or $T \times LA$. However, to avoid compression failure, the strength of such sections is to be considered as that of balanced sections only, i.e.,

$$M_u = M_{u\,lim} = 0.36\, f_{ck} b x_{u\,lim}(d - 0.42\, x_{u\,lim})$$

Illustration 3.4: A reinforced concrete beam with a width of 400 mm and a total depth of 800 mm. Take the effective cover of 50 mm and the working moment as 200 kN-m. The grade of steel and concrete used are Fe 415 and M20, respectively. Check whether this applied moment is less than the moment carrying capacity of the beam.

Solution:

D = Effective depth = Overall depth - Effective cover

= (800-50)

=750 mm.

Design moment = Partial safety factor × Working moment

= (1.5 × 200) kN-m

=300 kN-m.

Limiting moment of resistance = $0.138 f_{ck} b d^2$ (For Fe 415)

= $0.138 \times 20 \times 400 \times 750^2$ kN-m

= 621 kN-m.

So applied moment (300 kN-m) < Limiting moment of resistance.

So, the applied moment is less than the moment carrying capacity of the beam.

Illustration 3.5: A beam is simply supported with a clear span of 7.5 m. Load over the beam is 30 kN/m (Excluding self-weight). Design the beam using the Limit State Method if M20 grade concrete and Fe 415 grade steel are used. Take the width of the section as 350 mm.

Solution:

Assume total depth(D) = Span/10 = 7500/10 mm = 750 mm.

Given live load (LL) = 30 kN/m.

Calculated dead load the section (DL)= 25 kN/m^3 × 0.35m × 0.75m

= 6.5 kN/m.

Total working load = DL+LL

= (30+6.5)

= 36.5 kN/m.

Total design load = Partial safety factor × Working load

= (1.5 × 36.5) kN/m

= 54.75 kN/m.

Maximum moment (or load) will come at the middle of the beam (M_u) = $wl^2/8$

$$= \frac{54.57 \times 7.5^2}{8}$$

= 384.96 kN-m.

For under reinforced section, $M_{u,lim} \geq Mu$

Or, $0.138\, f_{ck}bd^2 \geq 384.96$ kN-m

Or, $d \geq \sqrt{\left(\frac{384.96 \times 10^6}{0.138 \times 20 \times 350}\right)}$

Or, $d \geq 631.3$ mm

And we have provided effective depth = D – effective cover

= 750-30 mm

= 720 mm.

So, 720 mm ≥ 631.3 mm.

So, our taken 'd' is okay for the beam to be under-reinforced.

Area of steel = $0.5(f_{ck}/f_y)\,[1-\sqrt{(1-(4.6\,\frac{M_u}{f_{ck}bd^2}))}]bd$

$$= 0.5 \times \frac{20}{415}\,[1-\sqrt{(1-\frac{4.6 \times 384.96 \times 10^6}{20 \times 350 \times 720^2})}]\ 350 \times 720 \text{ mm}^2$$

= 1727 mm²

Now, let us provide 20 mm bars.

No. of bars required $= \dfrac{Area\ of\ steel\ required}{\frac{\pi}{4}\times 20^2}$

$= \dfrac{1727}{\frac{\pi}{4}\times 20^2}$

Let us provide 6 no. of bars,

So, area of steel provided $= \dfrac{6\times\pi}{4\times 20^2}$

$= 1884.95\ mm^2$

Let us check whether the reinforcement provided is sufficient or not:

$(A_{st\ min}/bd) = \dfrac{0.85}{f_y}$

$A_{st,min} = \dfrac{0.85\times 350\times 750}{415} = 516.14\ mm^2$

Maximum area of steel = 4% of bd

$= 0.04\times 350\times 750$

$= 10500\ mm^2$.

So, $A_{st,min}$ (516.14 mm^2) < $A_{st,provided}$ (1884.95 mm^2) < $A_{st,max}$ (10500 mm^2)

Hence Ok.

Illustration 3.6: Find the ultimate moment of resistance of the reinforced concrete beam, which has a width of 150 mm and an overall depth of 300 mm and is reinforced with 3 no. of 16 mm diameter bars. The effective cover to the reinforcement is 50 mm. The cube strength of concrete used is 200 kg/cm^2, and the yield stress of steel is 2200 kg/cm^2.

Solution:

Characteristics compressive strength of concrete $f_{ck} = 200\ kg/cm^2 = 20\ N/mm^2$

Yield strength of steel $= f_y = 2200\ kg/cm^2 = 220\ N/mm^2$.

Depth of neutral axis = $(\frac{0.87 f_y A_{st}}{0.36 f_{ck} b})$ = $(\frac{0.87 \times 220 \times 3 \times \frac{\pi}{4} \times 16^2}{0.36 \times 20 \times 150})$

= 106.899 mm

Limiting depth of neutral axis = $[\frac{700}{1100+0.87 f_y}]d$ = $[\frac{700}{1100+(0.87 \times 220)}](300 - 50) = 135.511$

mm

So, the depth of the neutral axis is less than the critical depth. Hence, it is under-reinforced section.

Moment of resistance = $0.36 f_{ck} b X_u (d - 0.42 X_u)$

$= 0.36 \times 20 \times 150 \times 106.899 \times (250 - 0.42 \times 106.899)$ N-mm

$= 23.679 \times 10^6$ N-mm

= 23.679 kN-m.

Illustration 3.7: A doubly reinforced beam of size 250 mm width and 450 mm total depth is reinforced with 4 bars of 25 mm diameter on the tension side and 4 bars of 18 mm diameter on the compression side. The effective cover on the top and bottom of the beam is 50 mm. Garde of concrete used is M25, and the grade of steel used is Fe 250. Find the ultimate moment of resistance of the beam.

Solution:

Area of steel in tension = $\frac{4\pi}{4 \times 25^2}$ = 1963.49 mm^2

Area of steel in compression = $\frac{4\pi}{4 \times 18^2}$ = 1017.87 mm^2

Limiting depth of neutral axis for Fe 250 grade of steel = $0.53d = 0.53(450 - 50) = 212$ mm.

As we know, for balanced section:

$C_1 + C_2 = T$

$0.36 f_{ck} b X_u + A_{sc}(f_{sc} - f_{cc}) = 0.87 f_y A_{st}$

$(0.36 \times 20 \times 250 \times X_u) + 1017.8(0.87 \times 250 - 0.45 \times 20) = 0.87 \times 250 \times 1963.49$

$X_u = 119.35 \text{ mm} < X_{u\,lim}$

So, the section is under-reinforced.

So, ultimate moment of resistance = $0.36f_{ck}bX_u(d - 0.42X_u) + A_{sc}(f_{sc} - f_{cc})$ (d-effective cover)

= [0.36 × 20 × 250 × 119.35{400 - (0.42 × 119.35)}] + [1017.87{(0.87 × 415) - (0.45 × 20)}(400 - 50)]

= 149.44 kN-m.

Illustration 3.8: The design moment on the beam is given as 190 kN-m for a singly reinforced beam section. The grade of steel used is Fe 250, and the grade of concrete used is M20. The width of the section is 250, and the total depth is 500 mm. Take an effective cover of 50 mm on both the tension and compression sides. If dimension changes in the beam are restricted, check whether the beam should be transformed into a doubly reinforced beam.

Solution:

For Fe 250 grade of steel, the ultimate moment of resistance

$= 0.148 f_{ck} bd^2 = 0.148 \times 20 \times 250 \times (500\text{-}50)^2$

$= 149.85 \times 10^6$ N-mm

= 149.85 kN-m

So, the design moment (190 kN-m) is greater than the beam's maximum moment carrying capacity (149.85 kN-m).

We must provide a doubly reinforced beam since we cannot change width or effective depth due to dimension restrictions.

Illustration 3.9: For Illustration 3.8, calculate the area of steel required for the compression zone.

Solution:

Area of steel required for the compression zone $= \dfrac{Mu - Mu_{lim}}{(f_{sc} - f_{cc})(d - effective\ cover)}$

$$= \frac{(190-149.85)\times 10^6}{[(0.87\times 250)-(0.45\times 20)]\times(450-50)}$$

$= 481.414\ mm^2$.

3.5 DESIGN OF DOUBLY REINFORCED SECTION

3.5.1 Introduction of Doubly Reinforced Section

In reinforced concrete design, beams are essential for load-bearing. While singly reinforced beams suffice for many cases, doubly reinforced beams are required for greater demands. These beams are reinforced in both tension and compression zones, enhancing their capacity under stress.

Concrete effectively resists compression but is tensile weak. Singly reinforced beams contain steel only in the tension zone to prevent cracking. However, heavier loads or slender designs necessitate additional reinforcement. Doubly reinforced beams include steel in both zones to improve load capacity.

The primary benefit of doubly reinforced beams is their enhanced resistance to bending moments. By reinforcing the compression zone, these beams accommodate limited depth and insufficient tension reinforcement. This design increases strength without major size alterations, suitable for complex structures and heavy loads.

Ultimately, doubly reinforced beams merge steel and concrete strengths in both zones, providing an efficient solution for challenging structural needs. Engineers must grasp its design and applications for demanding projects.

In addition to this, a doubly reinforced beam is also utilized in the subsequent scenarios:

1. The external live loads may alternate i.e. may occur on either face of the member.
   Ex: In areas vulnerable to earthquakes, beams in structures must withstand forces that alter direction during seismic events, alternating between tension and compression on various faces of the beam.
2. The applied loads may be eccentric or move from one side of the beam to the other, resulting in uneven stress across the member.
3. The member may be subjected to a shock or impact on accidental lateral thrust.

Ex: In constructions such as railway bridges or loading platforms, where the beam may confront abrupt heavy loads or impacts from vehicles or machinery, additional reinforcement is essential to avert damage and ensure stability.

3.5.2 Doubly Reinforced Section in Flexure

R.C. beams with steel reinforcement on both tensile and compression sides are called doubly reinforced beams. The situation in which the doubly reinforced section is to be used is listed below:

- From architectural or any other construction problem, the depth of the R.C. beam is restricted.
- In some cases, the bending moment at the section changes the sign due to variation in loading; some of examples of such situations are:

  (a) Due to moving load in continuous beams

  (b) In precast members during handling

  (c) In bracing members of frames due to changes in the direction of wind loads.
- To improve the ductility of beams in earthquake regions.
- To reduce long-term deflection

Fig.3.5 shows the typical R.C. beams of doubly reinforced sections along with the strain and the stress variation along the depth.

The compressive steel of area A_{sc} is provided at an effective cover d' from extreme compression fibre. Let the stress in this steel be f_{sc}. Then, total compressive force is given by

$$C = C_c + C_s$$

Where Cc is the compressive force in concrete, and C_s is the compressive force in steel.

$$C_c = 0.36 f_{ck} b x_u - f_{cc} A_{sc}$$

Where, f_{cc} is the compressive stress in concrete at the level of compression steel and the term $f_{cc}A_{sc}$ represents the reduction of compressive forces due to the removal of concrete for placing compressive steel. Compared to other terms in assembling the compressive forces, this term is negligibly small. Hence, this term is neglected. Thus,

$$C_c = 0.36 f_{ck} b x_u$$

$$\text{Now, } C_s = f_{sc} Asc$$

$$\text{and } T = 0.87\, f_y Ast,$$

In the design, only the yielded condition of tensile steel is considered, but in case steel has not yielded (over-reinforced section), it can be found, as shown in the analysis of the reinforced section. By equating compressive and tensile forces to get equilibrium, we have

$$C = T$$

$$0.36 f_{ck} b x_u + f_{sc} Asc = 0.87\, f_y Ast$$

From the above equation x_u can be found. The following procedure may be followed to find the stress in compression steel:

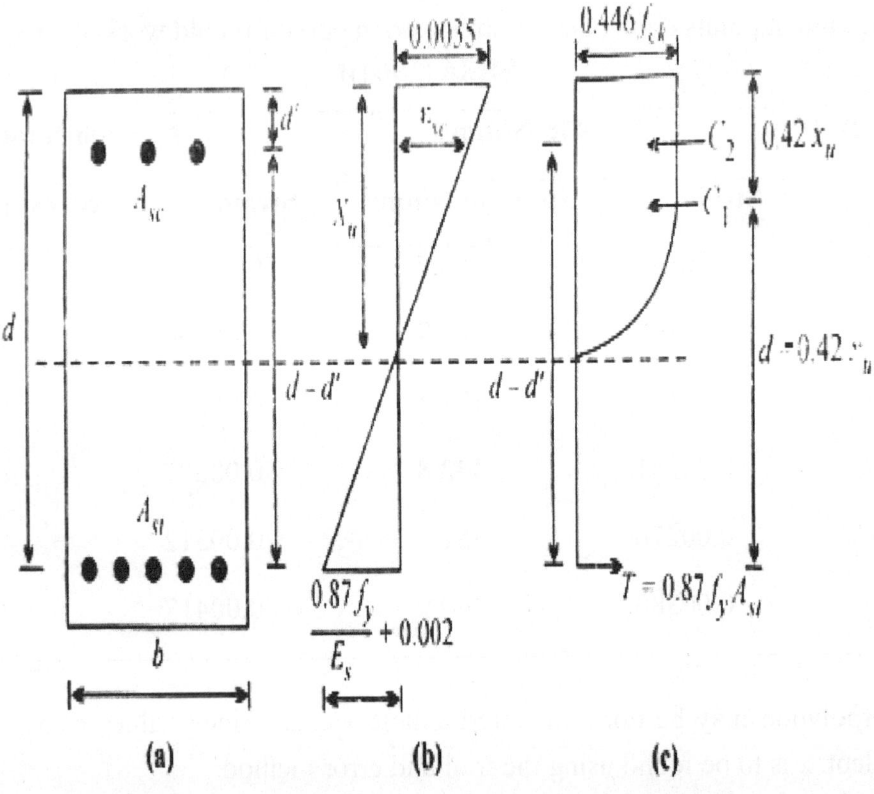

Figure 3.5: Diagram of doubly reinforced beam section

From the strain diagram at failure, the strain at the level of compression steel

$$\varepsilon_{sc} = 0.0035\,\frac{x_u - d'}{x_u} = 0.0035\left(1 - \frac{d'}{x_u}\right)$$

where d' = Distance of centroid of compression steel from the extreme compression fibre of concrete

In practical situations, d' is expressed in the ratio *(d'/d)*, which varies from 0.05 to 0.2.

The corresponding stress in compression steel may be obtained from the stress-strain curve of steel SP-16, which gives the following Table 3.4 for Fe 415 and Fe 500 steel as an extract of their stress-strain curves.

Table 3.5: Salient points on the design stress-strain curve for cold worked bars (Table A of SP-16 (1964))

Stress Level	f_y = 415 N/mm²		f_y = 500 N/mm²	
	Strain	**Stress in N/mm²**	**Strain**	**Stress in N/mm²**
$0.80f_y$	0.00144	288.7	0.00174	347.8
$0.85f_y$	0.00163	306.7	0.00194	369.6
$0.90f_y$	0.00192	324.8	0.00226	391.3
$0.95f_y$	0.00241	342.8	0.00277	413.0
$0.975f_y$	0.00276	351.8	0.00312	423.9
$1f_y$	0.00380	360.9	0.00417	434.8

Note:

Linear interpolation may be done for intermediate values. Since values of x_u and f_y are interdependent, x is to be found using the trial and error method.

However, in the case of mild steel, a direct relation can be established since the idealised stress-strain is linear up to f_y and then it is constant f_y.

Hence, for mild steel:

$$f_{sc} = \varepsilon_{sc} E_s$$
$$= 0.0035\left(1 - \frac{d\prime}{x_u}\right) 2 \times 10^5$$
$$= 700\left(1 - \frac{d\prime}{x_u}\right),$$

subjected to a maximum of stress of 0.87 f_y.

Illustration 3.10: Determine the ultimate moment of resistance of a doubly reinforced beam having a width of 300 mm and a total depth of 600 mm. The area of steel in tension is 2060 mm^2, and in compression is 804 mm^2. The effective cover for both tension and compression is 50 mm. The grade of concrete used is M20, and the steel grade is Fe 415.

Solution:

Effective cover = 50 mm, Effective depth = d = 600 – 50 = 550 mm

$X_{u,lim}$ = 0.48d = 0.48 × 550 = 264 mm

0.36 × 20 × 300 × X_u + 804(f_{sc} - 0.45 × 20) = 0.87 × 415 × 2060..........(i)

Trial 1: Assume f_{sc} = 350 N/mm^2 (0.87f_y)

By putting the above value of f_{sc} in equation (i), we get X_u = 217.4 mm

Strain in steel in compression zone = 0.0035[1-(effective cover/Xu)] = 0.035[1 - $\frac{50}{217.4}$] =0.00269

Find stress (f_{sc}) corresponding to strain 0.00269 from Table 3.4, which comes out to be 350.2 N/mm^2.

So, for the subsequent trial, consider f_{sc}= 350.2 N/mm^2.

Trial 2: Assuming f_{sc} = 350.2 N/mm^2,

The depth of the neutral axis=217.3 mm, and the corresponding fsc from Table 3.4, after calculating strain in steel in the compression zone, also comes out 350.2 N/mm^2.

Hence, our trial is successful.

Take X_u = 217.3 mm < $X_{u,lim}$ (264 mm). Hence under-reinforced.

So, ultimate moment of resistance= 0.36f_{ck} b X_u (d-0.42X_u) + A_{sc} (f_{sc} - f_{cc})

= 0.36 × 20 × 300 × 217.3[550-(0.42 × 217.3)] + 804[350.2-(0.45 × 20)](550-50)

$= 352.47 \times 10^6$ N-mm

$= 352.47$ kN-m

3.5.3 Limiting Moment of Resistance

The limiting moment of resistance can be obtained when x_u reaches x_{ulim} and; in that case, the limiting moment of resistance of the doubly reinforced beam section is given by:

$$M_{ulim} = 0.36f_{ck}bx_{ulim}(d - 0.42x_{ulim}) + (f_{sc} - 0.45f_{ck})A_{sc}(d - d')$$

Here, the values of f_{sc} depend on the strain in compression steel (ε_{sc}). When $x_u = x_{ulim}$, f_{sc} can be calculated by interpolation from Table 3.5 for different *(d′/d)* ratios.

Table 3.6: Values of f_{sc}, when $x_u = x_{ulim}$ for different d'/d ratios

Grade of steel	d′/d			
	0.05	**0.1**	**0.15**	**0.2**
Fe 250	217.5	217.5	217.5	217.5
Fe 415	355.1	351.9	342.4	329.2
Fe 500	423.9	411.3	395.1	370.3

3.5.4 Design Steps for a Given Factored Moment (M_u)

Determine A_{st}

For a given rectangular beam section (i.e., given b, d, f_{ck}, f_y), determine the limiting moment of resistance of a singly reinforced section (which is $0.148\, f_{ck}\, bd^2$ and $0.133\, f_{ck}\, bd^2$ for Fe 250, Fe 415 and Fe 500 respectively). If $M_{u\,lim}$ is greater than or equal to the factored moment M_u, then the section is designed singly reinforced. If M_u is greater than $M_{u\,lim}$, then the section is designed as a doubly reinforced section. Assume a suitable value of d' and determine ΔA_{st}; the total $A_{streqd.}$ can be obtained ($A_{st\,lim} + \Delta A_{st}$)

Determine A_{sc}

Using the value of ΔA_{st} provided, determine the value of $A_{sc\ reqd}$ from the expression of A_{sc}. The stress value in compression steel *(f_{sc})* is obtained from the strain value in compression steel *(ε_{sc})*. The compression bars should be so selected that the area of compression steel provided is as close to the required compression steel.

Illustration 3.11: For the above question, calculate the steel required for the compression zone.

Solution:

$$\text{Area of steel required for the compression zone} = \frac{Mu - Mu_{lim}}{(f_{sc} - f_{cc})(d - effective\ cover)}$$

$$= \frac{(190 - 149.85) \times 10^6}{[(0.87 \times 250) - (0.45 \times 20)] \times (450 - 50)}$$

$$= 481.414 \text{ mm}^2$$

SUMMARY

A reinforced concrete beam is a crucial structural element, supporting shear and bending stresses and transferring loads from slabs to walls or columns. The design process for reinforced concrete beams involves determining design loads and load combinations, calculating the bending moment and shear force, selecting an appropriate beam cross-section, assuming preliminary reinforcement, checking for deflection, checking for cracking, detailing longitudinal reinforcement, providing shear reinforcement if necessary, and determining bar spacing and anchorage. The design is carried out for the most critical loading conditions, ensuring the beam can withstand maximum loads without failure. The beam's dimensions are chosen based on the bending moment and shear force, and the minimum steel ratio and maximum spacing of reinforcement are checked. The final design and checks ensure all design criteria are met, including strength, stability, deflection, and crack control, and the reinforcement provided is within the limits specified by IS 456-2000.

EXERCISE

Make a few groups of students, each having five students. The students are assigned to plan and design the parking shed for a small community centre. The shed will accommodate 10 cars and must provide shelter from rain and sun. Design the required RCC beams for the shed.

MULTIPLE CHOICE QUESTIONS

1. The acceptable limit for the safety and serviceability requirements before failure occurs is called
   A) Breaking point
   B) Failure point
   C) Limit state
   D) Ductility
2. The partial safety factor to be used in limiting the state of deflection for the strength of concrete is
   A) 1.2
   B) 1.5
   C) 1.0
   D) 0.8
3. In limit state design of concrete structures, the recommended partial safety factor 'γ_m' for steel according to IS 456-2000 is
   A) 1.5
   B) 1.15
   C) 1.0
   D) 0.87
4. The design strength of steel in limit state design is
   A) $f_y/1.5$
   B) $f_y/0.87$
   C) $0.87f_y$
   D) $0.27f_y$
5. The minimum grade of concrete recommended for severe climatic conditions as per IS 456-2000 is
   A) M40
   B) M30
   C) M35
   D) M20
6. The minimum nominal cover to reinforcement recommended for very severe climatic conditions as per IS 456-2000 is:
   A) 30 mm
   B) 75 mm
   C) 45 mm

D) 50 mm

7. A beam of width 300 mm and effective depth of 500 mm of M25 concrete is subjected to a factored flexure moment of 100 kN-m. The depth of the neutral axis of the beam is:
   A) 79 mm
   B) 265.5 mm
   C) 240 mm
   D) 50 mm
8. The depth of a rectangular portion of the stress block of concrete in compression is
   A) 3/7 x_u
   B) 4/7 x_u
   C) 2/7 x_u
   D) x_u

ANSWERS TO MULTIPLE CHOICE QUESTIONS

1	2	3	4	5	6	7	8
C	C	B	C	B	D	A	A

SHORT ANSWER TYPE QUESTIONS

1. What do you understand by 'Limit State'?
2. Write down various assumptions of singly reinforced design of design.
3. Find the area of the cross-sectional area of reinforcement if the 6 bars of 6 mm radius are used.
4. What do you mean by stress bock parameter derive?
5. Write down the procedure to design a singly reinforced beam.
6. Determine the neutral axis depth of a 250 x 350 mm beam section reinforced with 3 – 20 mm diameter bars of Fe 250 grade steel. The beam comprises M20 concrete, and the effective cover to reinforcement is 50 mm.
7. Determine the ultimate moment of resistance of a rectangular beam of width 300 mm with 550 mm effective depth, which is cast with M30 grade of concrete and reinforced with four numbers of 25 mm diameter bars and Fe 250 steel grade.

LONG ANSWER TYPE QUESTIONS

1. Design a rectangular beam of section 230 mm x 600 mm with an effective span of 6m. The imposed load on the beam is 40 kN/m^2 using M20 concrete and 415 steel.
2. A reinforced concrete beam 200 mm X 400 mm effective depth is used over an effective span of 5m. It is subjected to a uniformly distributed load of 7 kN/m, including its weight.

Find the necessary steel reinforcement at the centre of the span. Take allowable stresses in steel and concrete as 130 N/mm^2 and 4N/mm^2, respectively.

3. Design an R.C. beam to carry a load of 6 kN/m inclusive of its weight on an effective span of 6 m. Keep the breadth to be 2/3rd of effective depth. The permissible stresses in concrete and steel do not exceed 5 N/mm^2 and 140 N/mm^2, respectively.
4. Write down the fundamental assumptions of the Working Stress Method and Limit State Method.

TUTORIAL

A college corridor has a beam that spans 6 meters and supports an RC slab. The slab is 120 mm thick, and the corridor is expected to experience heavy foot traffic. The beam also supports a 1.2 m high parapet wall (230mm thick) on one side.

- Calculate the loads from the slab and parapet wall.
- Determine the live load based on a heavily trafficked area.
- Design the beam, checking for bending and shear capacity.

Assume data accordingly.

KNOW MORE

For more information related to this topic, scan the QR code.

OR

Type this link in your browser

https://archive.nptel.ac.in/courses/105/105/105105105/

BIBLIOGRAPHY

1. Kandekar, S.B., Talikoti, R.S. (2018) *Study of torsional behaviour of reinforced concrete beams strengthened with aramid fibre strips*. *Int J Adv Struct Eng* 10(1), 465–474.

2. Krishna Raju, and N. Pranesh, R.N. (2018). *Reinforced Concrete Design Principles and Practice*, New Age International: Mumbai.

3. Pillai, S.U., and Menon, D. (2017). *Reinforced Concrete Design*, McGraw Hill Publications: New Delhi.

4. Sinha N.C., and Roy S.K. (2007). *Fundamentals of Reinforced Concrete*, S. Chand & Co.: New Delhi.

4 SHEAR, BOND, AND DEVELOPMENT LENGTH IN THE DESIGN OF RCC MEMBER

UNIT SPECIFICS

In this unit, students will learn about the critical aspects of shear design in reinforced concrete (RCC) structures, starting with the concept of nominal shear stress and the design shear strength of concrete. The unit covers the design of shear reinforcement, including the minimum shear reinforcement requirements and the provisions outlined in IS 456. Students will explore various forms of shear reinforcement and understand how to calculate the adequacy of a section for shear using simple numerical problems. The unit also introduces the concept of bond, bond stress, and the methods to check bond stress, including determining development length for tension and compression members. The importance of anchorage, including the value of a 90-degree hook and lapping of bars, is also discussed. Finally, students will be introduced to serviceability limit state checks, ensuring the structure remains functional and safe under service conditions. Students will gain a deeper understanding of shear design and reinforcement details in RCC structures through practical examples.

RATIONALE

The chapter on Shear, Bond, and Development Length in Design of RCC Members is essential for providing students with a comprehensive understanding of key concepts that ensure the safety and functionality of reinforced concrete structures. Shear and bond are critical factors in the design of concrete members, as they influence the overall structural performance, durability, and safety. By studying shear stress, shear strength, and the design of appropriate shear reinforcement, students learn how to prevent structural failure due to excessive shear forces. Additionally, understanding bond stress and development length is crucial for ensuring proper anchorage of reinforcement, vital in transferring forces between concrete and steel reinforcements. The provisions of IS 456 guide the design process, ensuring that the concrete member is safe and efficient under various loading conditions. This chapter emphasises practical applications with simple numerical examples, enabling students to develop the skills necessary to design RCC members that meet strength and serviceability requirements. By mastering these concepts, students will be better equipped to solve real-world engineering problems and contribute to the design of safe, durable reinforced concrete structures.

PRE-REQUISITE

Basic mathematics

UNIT OUTCOMES

The list of outcomes of this unit is as follows:

U4-O1: Understand the design shear strength of concrete

U4-O2: Check bond stress and determine development length

U4-O3: Computation of shear reinforcement

U4-O4: Limit state serviceability check of the RC members

Unit Outcomes	Expected Mapping with Course Outcomes (1- Weak correlation; 2- Medium correlation; 3- Strong correlation)				
	CO-1	CO-2	CO-3	CO-4	CO-5
U4-O1	2	2	2	-	2
U4-O2	1	1	3	-	3
U4-O3	-	2	3	-	3
U4-O4	1	3	1	-	2

4.1 SHEAR FORCE

Shear force can be defined as the force which acts tangentially on the body. The reason behind this is the tangential component of the force parallel to a body's planar cross-section. Due to the effect of shear force, the cross-section of the body can be deformed. For example, the wind force is applied to the side walls of a building, and transverse force is applied to beams. To resist the externally applied shear force, opposite internal forces develop inside the body as a reaction. When a body is subjected to two equal and opposite forces acting tangentially, it results in deformation in the body, causing a corresponding strain known as shear strain.

Due to shear force, bending occurs in the structural element. Generally, shear bending also comes into action, which may lead to the failure of the structure. So, we must ensure that the structural beams and other members are safe in shear.

4.1.1 Types of Shear

There are three types of shears:

Flexural shear

This kind of shear is generated due to flexure or bending. Shear due to a change in bending moment along the span is known as flexural shear. Beams are usually subjected to flexural shear.

Typically, in beams, the bending moment increases near the centre. Fig.4.1 gives a simply supported beam subjected to a uniformly distributed load. As we move a minimal *'dx'* distance towards the centre, the value of the bending moment increases from *'M'* to *'M+dm.'* Due to this, the bending compression increased from *'C'* to *'C+dc,'* and bending tension increased from *'T'* to *'T+dt.'*

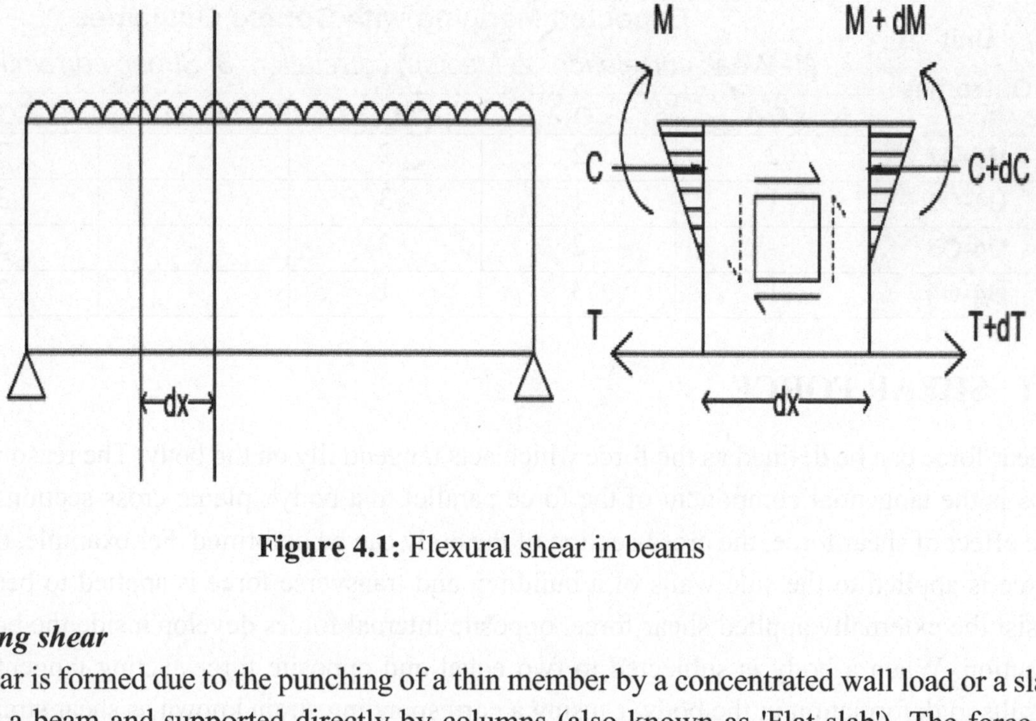

Figure 4.1: Flexural shear in beams

Punching shear

The shear is formed due to the punching of a thin member by a concentrated wall load or a slab without a beam and supported directly by columns (also known as 'Flat slab'). The force is developed parallel to the structure's surface (Fig.4.2). Footing slabs are also subjected to punching shear.

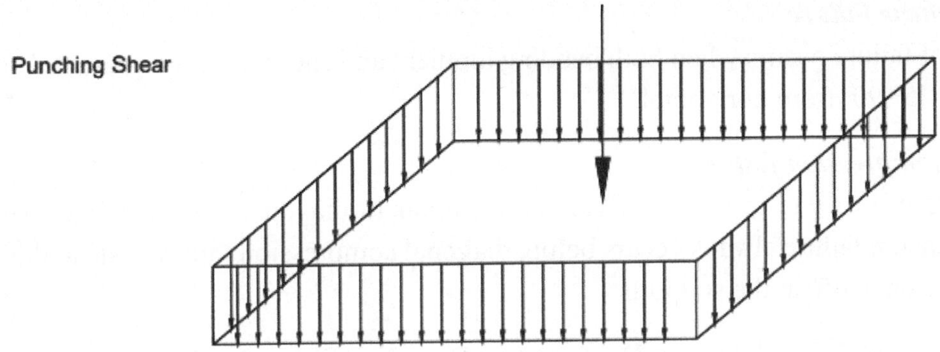

Figure 4.2: Punching shear

Torsional shear

The torque applied to an RCC member generates this kind of shear. In RCC structures, flexural shear generally accompanies torsional shear, as shown in Fig.4.3.

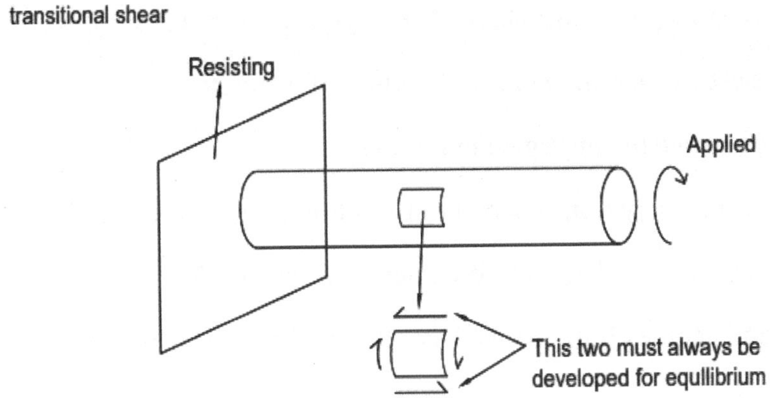

Figure 4.3: Torsional shear

Beams are usually subjected to flexural shear and sometimes to torsional shear. Flexural shear is called one-way shear, whereas punching shear is called two-way shear.

4.1.2 Modes of Failure Due to Shear in Structural Element

There are mainly three modes of failure due to shear:

Diagonal tension failure

This kind of failure is mainly seen where shear force is maximum, like the supports. Here, diagonal cracks are seen at 45° to the horizontal. The only reason behind this failure is the sheer force.

Flexural shear failure

This kind of failure occurs when both bending moment and shear force are present. Cracks are inclined at 45º-90º from horizontal.

Diagonal compression failure

This failure occurs due to a large shear force similar to diagonal tension failure. However, diagonal tension failure always occurs before diagonal compression failure. Due to this failure, cracks are seen at 45º at the supports.

4.1.3 Mechanism of Shear Resistance Developed in the Concrete Section

Shear resistance in concrete is developed by the various components with which it is composed. Concrete loses all its power after cracking. So, the different elements with which the shear resistance is developed are the uncracked portion of concrete, aggregate interlocking, reinforcement in the concrete, and the reinforcement provided to resist shear only.

The total strength of concrete against shear $(V_u) = V_c + V_{ay} + V_d + V_s$

Where V_c= Shear resistance by an uncracked portion of concrete.

V_{ay}= Shear resistance by aggregate interlocking.

V_d= Shear resistance by reinforcement in addition to its dowel action.

V_s = Shear resistance by shear reinforcement (i.e., stirrups).

Sometimes, the load becomes high, so we have to introduce shear reinforcement in the form of shear.

Suppose a total load of 100 kN is applied on a particular section as shear. Uncracked portion V_c first takes the load. When the section starts to break, the load is shifted to V_{ay} and V_d, and finally, when all three have failed, the load is resisted by shear reinforcement:

$$V_u = V_c + V_{ay} + V_d + V_s$$

$$100 = 20 + 30 + 30 + 20$$

Before flexural cracks, only V_c develops. After the commencement of crack, both V_{ay} and V_d developed. Additional shear force is taken by shear reinforcement (V_s), which is nothing more than 'stirrups'.

4.1.4 Design Shear Strength of Concrete

The design shear strength of concrete is defined as the ability to resist forces mainly responsible for the sliding or shearing of its inner structure. Various factors affect the design shear strength of concrete, such as grade of concrete, percentage of tensile reinforcement, compressive strength of concrete, and percentage of shear reinforcement. The design shear strength of concrete varies with the presence of shear reinforcement. Shear reinforcement means the provision or design of reinforcement for resisting shear force.

Without shear reinforcement (Clause 40 of IS 456-2000)

In this section, we will only discuss the shear-resisting power of the concrete portion. This strength is denoted by T_c, (from Table 4.1) which is a function of the grade of concrete and the percentage of tensile steel.

Under no circumstances should the nominal shear stress in beams T_v not exceed T_{cmax} given in Table 4.2 for different grades of concrete.

Table 4.1: For design shear strength of concrete without shear reinforcement (Table 19 of IS 456-2000)

P_t=(A_{st}/bd) x 100	M15	M20	M25
<0.15	0.28	0.28	0.29
0.25	0.35	0.35	0.36
0.50	0.46	0.48	0.49
0.75	0.54	0.56	0.57
1	0.60	0.62	0.64

Table 4.2: For maximum compressive shear stress in concrete (Table 20 of IS 456-2000)

Grade	M15	M20	M25	M30	M35	>M40
T_{cmax}	2.5	2.8	3.1	3.5	3.7	4.0

With shear reinforcement

Here, the maximum compressive stress (T_{cmax}) and design shear strength of concrete are taken into care, which is a function of the grade of concrete only. Under any circumstances, the shear stress acting on the beam should not exceed T_{cmax} to prevent diagonal compression failure.

Under any circumstances, the applied shear stress should always be less than the concrete's maximum compressive shear stress. The applied shear stress may or may not be less than the design shear strength of concrete, and if it exceeds the design shear strength of concrete, then shear reinforcement should be provided for the additional shear force.

4.1.5 Critical Sections for Shear in Different Types of Beam

While designing a concrete member for shear, we must see where the shear force is critical for the section. The critical section must be located where the shear force reaches its maximum value and/or the cross-section area is minimum. The locations of critical sections for some types of beams are given below:

Simply supported beam

In a simply supported beam, the critical section is at a distance of *'d'* from the face of support, where *'d'* is the effective depth of the beam. In Fig.4.4, of a cross-section of a simply supported beam, the arrows represent the direction of shear force. Fig.4.4 shows the average shear stress distribution below the beam's neutral axis in the adjacent figure of the simply supported beam. Since the concrete below the neutral axis is assumed to be cracked during balanced failure, stress is considered constant, which is the reason behind the uniform nature of the arrows in the diagram.

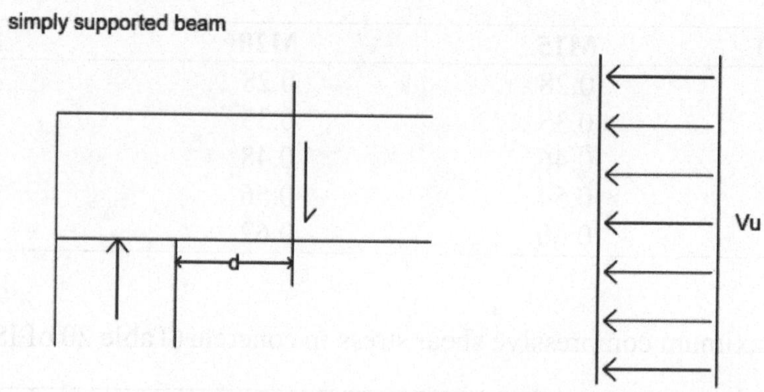

Figure 4.4: Critical section for shear in a simply supported beam

Cantilever beam

In the cantilever beam, the critical section is at the face of the support. In Fig.4.5, the arrows represent the direction of shear force in the two connected members.

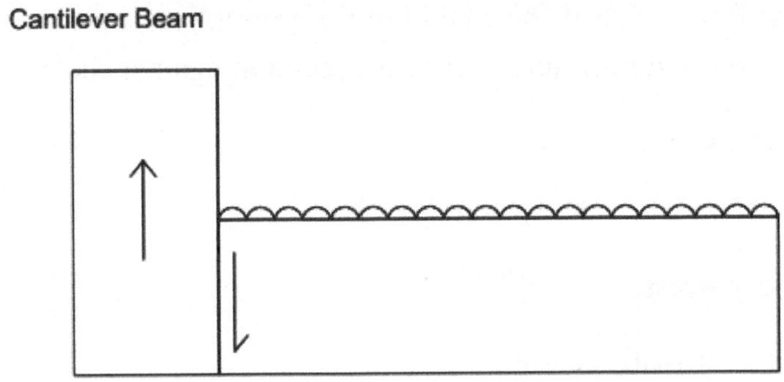

Figure 4.5: Critical section for shear in a cantilever beam

Beam-column joint

In a beam-column joint, the critical section is developed at a distance *'d'* from the column on both sides (Fig.4.6), where *'d'* is the effective depth of the beam.

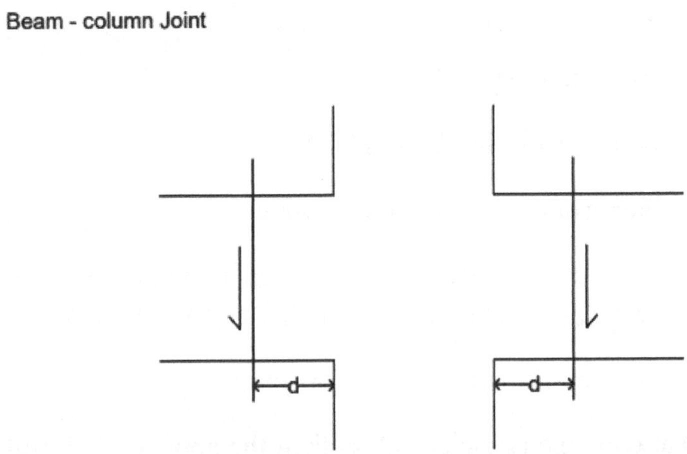

Figure 4.6: Critical section for shear in a beam-column joint

4.1.6 Design Steps for Shear Reinforcement

Several steps are involved in checking whether structural elements can withstand the applied shear force. If the stress generated due to the applied shear force is well within the shear strength of concrete, then only minimum shear reinforcement, as per the codal provision, is provided. However, when the applied shear force exceeds the shear strength of concrete, the shear reinforcement takes additional shear force. Shear reinforcement is the reinforcement or steel used to take the shear force. As mentioned earlier, in no case should the stress generated due to the applied shear force exceed the maximum compressive stress of concrete. Given below are the steps involved in designing shear reinforcement against shear:

1. Calculate nominal/average shear stress-

$$V_u = T_v(bd) \qquad 4.1$$

T_v= Nominal/average shear stress,

V_u= Factored shear force at critical section,

b = Width of the section,

d= effective depth of the section.

2. Check whether $T_v < T_{c\,max}$ to avoid diagonal compression failure.

$T_{c\,max}$= Maximum shear resistance of concrete irrespective of whether there is shear reinforcement.

If $T_v > T_{c\,max}$, then we have two options:

- Redesign the section by increasing '*b*' and '*d*'. Or,
- Increase $T_{c\,max}$ by increasing the grade of concrete.

3. The next step is to find the design shear strength of concrete (T_c), a function of the steel percentage and the concrete grade. Find its value from Table 19 of IS 456-2000.

4. If $T_v < T_c$, provide minimum shear reinforcement for safety.

5. If $T_v > T_c$, it is clear that concrete capacity is less than the applied load. So, it is confirmed that there will be diagonal tension failure, so shear reinforcement will be provided.

There is an additional stress (T_v-T_c), for which reinforcement is required.

6. The concrete portion will take total shear force and the shear reinforcements, also known as stirrups:

$V_u = V_{concrete} + V_{stirrup}$

Where

$V_{concrete}$= It is the shear force taken by the concrete portion,

$V_{stirrup}$= It is the shear force taken by shear reinforcements or stirrups.

$V_u = T_c(bd)+V_{stirrup}$

From Eq. 4.1, we can write:

$T_v(bd)=T_c(bd) + V_{stirrup}$

$V_{stirrup}=(T_v-T_c)\ bd.$

Shear reinforcement or stirrups must be designed for the force of $V_{stirrup}=(T_v-T_c)\ bd$ for the $T_v>T_c$ case.

4.1.7 Types of Shear Reinforcement

There are three main types of shear reinforcement seen in the beams. The shear strength of the reinforced concrete section can be enhanced by providing shear reinforcement in any of the three forms mentioned below:

Vertical stirrups

These stirrups are provided to prevent the cracks from increasing due to shear force (Fig.4.7)

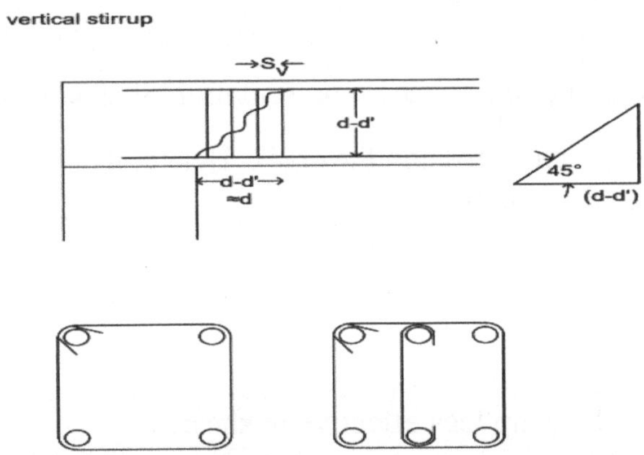

Figure 4.7: Vertical stirrups

There are two main types of vertical stirrup – 2-legged stirrup and 3-legged stirrup. Since stirrups are provided to resist the cracks, no stirrups crossing one crack=(d/S_v), where *'d'* is the effective depth of the beam and *'S_v'* is the stirrup spacing along the length of the member. If *'S_v'* decreases, the number of shear reinforcements increases.

Now, let us calculate the maximum shear force that stirrups can resist. Since the RC members are designed for ductile failure, not sudden failure, the shear reinforcement is also designed for yielding. Hence, at the limit state of shear, the vertical component of shear resisted by stirrup legs is calculated as below:

Maximum stress can be generated in steel = $0.87f_y$, where f_y is the characteristic strength of the steel used as a stirrup.

So, the maximum force that can be resisted by one stirrup= $0.87f_y\ (A_{sv})$

A_{sv}= Area of shear reinforcement= $2x\ \pi/4\ x\ \varphi^2$ (For 2-legged vertical stirrup), where φ is the bar diameter.

$= 3\ x\ \pi/4\ x\ \varphi^2$ (For 3-legged vertical stirrup)

Now, if we consider the equilibrium of vertical forces across a potential diagonal crack, which is assumed to extend at an angle of 45° with the axis of the beam (as shown in Fig.4.8).

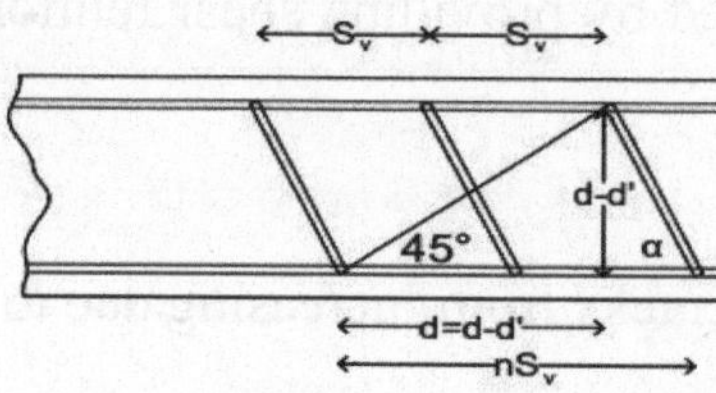

Figure 4.8: Schematic diagram for the representation of spacing of stirrups

Let *'n'* be several shear reinforcements crossing the crack. Hence, the total vertical shear force resisted in one crack width, V_{us}, is given by:

$V_{us}= nA_{sv}\ 0.87f_y sin\alpha$

where

A_{sv}= Total cross-sectional area of stirrup legs effective in shear,

f_y= characteristic strength of the stirrup reinforcement, which shall not be taken greater than 415 N/mm².

From the above figure,

$nS_v=(d-d`)\ cot45^o+(d-d`)\ cot\alpha$

$=(d-d`)\ (cot45^o+cot\alpha)$

$=(d-d`)\ (1+cot\alpha)$

$=d(1+cot\alpha)$

$V_{us}=d(1+cot\alpha)\ A_{sv}0.87f_y sin\alpha/S_v$

For vertical stirrups $\alpha = 90^o$

So, shear that can be resisted by shear reinforcement as vertical stirrup =

$$V_{us}=0.87f_yA_{sv}(d/S_v \qquad 4.2$$

Generally, a mild steel bar (Fe 250) is used in stirrups since it is easy to bend.

According to Clause 26.5.1.5 of IS 456-2000, the maximum spacing between consecutive vertical stirrups is a minimum of the following:

- 0.75d
- S_v<300 mm
- Find spacing from minimum shear reinforcement criteria.
- Find spacing from the V_{us} formula in Eq. 4.2

Inclined stirrups

Inclined stirrups are better than vertical stirrups since cracks are generally inclined at some angle (Fig.4.9). So, the stirrups become perpendicular to the cracks, which is suitable for resistance.

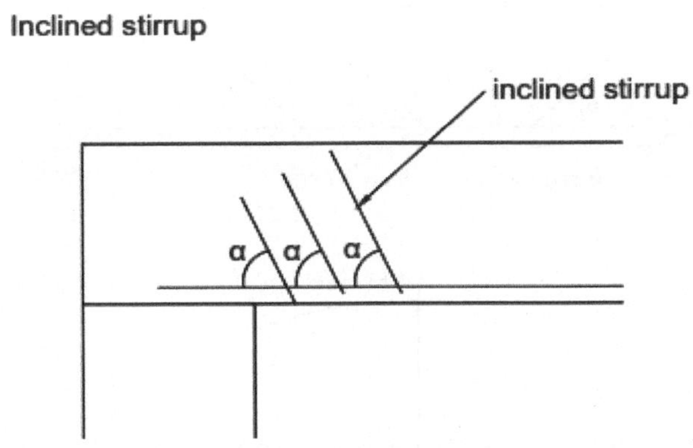

Figure 4.9: Inclined stirrup

Total shear that can be resisted by shear reinforcement as inclined stirrup =

$$0.87 f_y A_{sv} (d/S_v)(\sin\alpha + \cos\alpha) \tag{4.3}$$

Where $'\alpha'$ is the inclination angle of the stirrups concerning the horizontal. Generally, it is inclined at 45°.

The stirrup requirement is less in an inclined stirrup than vertical stirrups since it covers more distance.

According to Clause 26.5.1.5 of IS 456-2000, the maximum spacing between consecutive inclined stirrups is a minimum of the following:

- d (Since inclined stirrups are better than vertical so, total $'d'$ is taken)
- S_v<300 mm
- Find spacing from the minimum shear reinforcement criteria
- Find spacing from the V_{us} formula above in Eq. 4.2

Bent up bars

Here, stirrups are not provided. Longitudinal bars (Fig.4.10) are bent to resist tension and carry the shear force at the support. Generally, near the centre of a beam, the bending moment is high, and as towards the support, the bending moment gradually decreases, and the shear force increases. That is why tensile reinforcement is reduced, and bars are bent up.

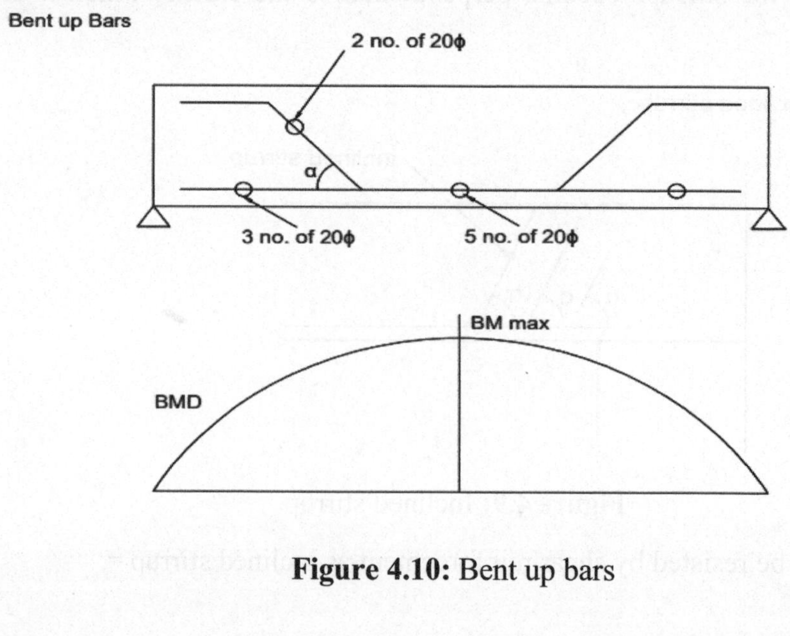

Figure 4.10: Bent up bars

As per Clause 40.4 of IS 456-2000, the shear resistance contribution of bent-up bars shall not be more than 50% of the $(T_v\text{-}T_c)\ bd$, and a vertical or inclined stirrup should resist the remaining shear.

Total shear that can be resisted by shear reinforcement as bent-up bars,

$V_{us} = 0.87 f_y A_{sv}(d/S_v)\ sin\alpha$ (when bars are bent up at same cross-section)

$V_{us} = 0.87 f_y A_{sv}(d/S_v)\ (sin\alpha + cos\alpha)$ (when bars are bent up at different cross-sections

Where 'α' is the angle of inclination of the bars with horizontal.

According to Clause 26.5.1.5 of IS 456-2000, the maximum spacing between consecutive vertical stirrups is a minimum of the following:

- $0.75d$
- S_v<300 mm
- Find spacing from minimum shear reinforcement criteria.
- Find spacing from the V_{us} formula given in Eq. 4.3

4.1.8 Minimum Shear Reinforcement Criteria

Minimum shear reinforcement is provided in the beams when the applied shear force is well within the shear strength of concrete. Minimum shear reinforcement in the beam is provided to ensure the following:

- To prevent sudden beam failure due to loss of bond between steel and concrete when the bursting of concrete cover occurs.
- To prevent brittle shear failure due to diagonal principal tension. It is internal tension due to a bending moment caused by shear force. The diagonal tension crack originates at an angle of 45° and breaks the beam into pieces.
- To reduce cracks due to shrinkage of concrete and thermal stresses.
- To hold the main reinforcement and increase the confinement

The formula for minimum shear reinforcement is as follows:

$(A_{sv}/bS_v) \geq (0.4/0.87 f_y)$

Even if $T_v < T_c$, always provide minimum shear reinforcement for safety.

Illustration 4.1 A beam has a width of 230 mm, an effective depth of 460 mm, and 5 number of 16 mm diameter bars as tensile reinforcement. The grade of concrete used is M20, and the steel grade is Fe 415. The factored shear force acting on the beam is 52.5 kN. Design the shear reinforcement of the beam using 2-legged 6 mm mild steel bars.

Solution:

I. Nominal shear stress acting on the beam $=Tv=V_u/bd$

$= (52.5 \times 10^3) / (230 \times 460)\ N/mm^2 = 0.4962\ N/mm^2$

II. For M20 grade of the concrete value of $T_{c\ max}$ from Table 20 of IS 456-2000 is 2.8 N/mm^2

So $T_v < T_{c\ max}$; Hence, safe in diagonal compression failure.

III. $P_t = (A_{st}/bd) \times 100 = (5 \times \pi/4 \times 16^2)/(230 \times 460) \times 100 = 0.9502\%$.

Table 19 of IS 456-2000 corresponds to 0.95% steel and M20 grade of concrete T_c=0.608 N/mm^2.

IV. T_v (0.4962) < T_c (0.608) So, concrete can withstand the given shear stress (V_u). So, it is also safe in diagonal compression failure.

So, we need to provide minimum shear reinforcement just for safety, Such as a 2-legged 6 mm mild steel (Fe 250) vertical stirrup.

$$A_{sv}/bS_v \geq 0.4/(0.87f_y)$$

$$(2 \times \pi/4 \times 6^2)/(230 \times S_v) \geq 0.4 / (0.87 \times 250)$$

$$S_v \leq 133.68\ mm.$$

V. Calculation of spacing:

- 0.75d=0.75 × 460=345 mm.
- 300 mm
- From minimum shear reinforcement criteria, 133.68 mm = Rounded off to 130 mm

Taking a minimum of the above three spacings provides a 2-legged mild steel vertical stirrup at 130 mm centre-to-centre distance.

Illustration 4.2 Suppose in Illustration 4.2, the factored shear force is given as 90 kN. Now, redesign the shear reinforcement.

Solution:

I. $T_v = (90 \times 10^2)/(230 \times 460) = 0.85$ N/mm^2.

II. $T_{c\,max} = 2.8$ N/mm^2 (Independent of applied shear force). So, $T_v < T_{c\,max}$. So, it is safe in diagonal compression failure.

III. $T_c = 0.608$ N/mm^2 (Independent of applied shear force). So now $T_v > T_c$. So, it is not safe for diagonal tension failure. So, we need to design for shear reinforcement.

IV. $V_{us} = (T_v - T_c)\, bd = 0.87 f_y A_{sv} (d/S_v)$

$$(0.85-0.608) \times 230 \times 260 = 0.87 \times 250 \times 2 \times \pi/4 \times 6^2 \times (230/S_v)$$

$$S_v = 220.97 \text{ mm}$$

V. Calculation of spacing-

- 0.75d=0.75 × 460=345 mm
- 300 mm
- From minimum shear reinforcement criteria= 133.68 mm.= Rounded off to 130 mm
- From design for shear reinforcement=220.97 mm

Taking a minimum of the above spacings provides a 2-legged mild steel vertical stirrup at 130 mm centre-to-centre distance.

This analysis shows that spacing in minimum shear reinforcement is less than the spacing coming due to extra shear force. So, minimum shear reinforcement and shear resisting ability are already pretty much more than the extra shear stress that is acting

4.2 BOND AND ANCHORAGE

A bond is needed between steel and concrete so there is no relative movement, and steel reaches its yield stress without slipping. A sufficient bond is required between concrete and steel to prevent relative movement. An adequate reinforcement inside concrete is provided to utilise member strength without premature failure fully.

Reasons behind bond

- Adhesive force between concrete and steel.
- Frictional resistance.
- Mechanical resistance.

Typically, two types of reinforcement bars are there – plain (Fe 250) Fig.4.11 and ribbed or deformed (Fe 415 and Fe 500) Fig.4.12. The mechanical resistance of ribbed bars is generally 60% more than that of plain bars.

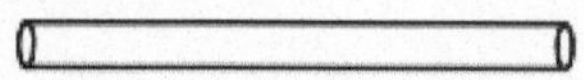

Figure 4.11: Plain bars (Typically Fe 250)

No mechanical resistance

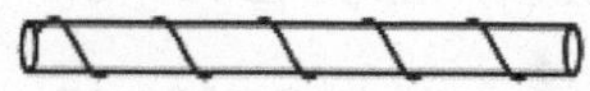

Figure 4.12: *Ribbed bars (Typically* Fe 415 and Fe 500)

With mechanical resistance

4.2.1 Bond Stress and Types of Bond Stress

In simple words, bond stress can be defined as the shear force per unit area. It develops between concrete and reinforcing steel or between different layers of concrete. Bond stress can be defined as the resistance to sliding between the concrete interface and embedded reinforcement. The various importance of bond stress is as follows:

- To transfer tensile forces from concrete to reinforcement.
- To ensure the structural integrity of reinforced concrete elements.
- To prevent slippage of the rebar within the concrete.

There are majorly two significant types of bond stress, which are discussed below:

Flexural bond stress

It is generated due to flexure or bending. Bending is generally more at the centre, and shear force gradually decreases near the centre for a supported beam. So, flexural bond stress decreases as we move closer to the middle of the beam. Since the shear force at the supports is the maximum bond stress, it will also be maximum there. Bond stress and its safety are checked at the beam's support.

The stress value due to applied shear should be less than permissible bond stress (in WSM) or design bond stress (in LSM).

Table 4.3: For design bond stress for plain bars in tension (Clause 26.2.1.1 of IS-456-2000)

Grade of concrete	M20	M25	M30	M35	>M40
T_{bd}	1.2	1.4	1.5	1.7	1.9

If $T<T_{bd}$, then no failure will occur.

Design bond stress is increased by 60% in the case of HYSD (Fe 415 and Fe 500) ribbed bars.

Bond stress is more due to end bearing.

Anchorage bond stress

Anchorage bond stress is developed around the bar to provide proper anchorage to reinforcement so that reinforcement attains its desired stress (i.e., 0.87 f_y). Anchorage bond stress is developed in the region where there is no change in bending moment. Sufficient anchorage length in 'Development length' is given inside concrete.

4.2.2 Development Length

Let us determine its value since we know that anchorage bond stress is developed along the development length. Whatever force is applied to the bar must be transformed from steel to concrete.

Force applied = Force transferred

$(0.87f_y) \times \pi/4 \times (\varphi^2) = T_{bd}\,(\pi\varphi L_d)$

where L_d is the development length.

$L_d = (0.87f_y\varphi)/\,(4T_{bd})$

Where T_{bd} is design bond stress for plain bars in tension.

When bond stress T_{bd} increases, we use HYSD (High Yielding Strength Deformed Steel) bars, and the development length can be shortened.

To understand development length, we need to understand the bundling of bars. When the number of bars is too high to accommodate the tension zone, most of the space is filled with steel, and there is very little space for aggregate. Then, we do a bundle of bars to provide space for aggregate. Bundling enhances the compaction of concrete. In the case of bundled bars, the value of the development length is increased.

Illustration 4.3 Find the development length for the HYSD bar of Fe 415 grade in the tension of 20 mm diameter in contact with the M20 grade of concrete

Solution:

$L_d = (0.87 f_y \varphi)/(4 T_{bd})$

$= (0.87 \times 415 \times 20)/ (4 \times 1.2 \times 1.6)$

(Since it is HYSD bar bond stress, T_{bd} in tension can be increased by 60%)

$= 940.23$ mm.

Illustration 4.4 Suppose the development length is asked for HYSD bars in compression in Illustration 4.3.

Solution:

The bond stress T_{bd} will be increased by 25%.

So, $L_d = (0.87 \times 415 \times 20)/ (4 \times 1.2 \times 1.6 \times 1.25) = 752.184$ mm.

We need a shorter bond length in compression.

4.2.3 Bond Failure

In simple words, bond failure means breaking the connection between concrete and steel. The various reasons behind the failure of the bond are discussed as follows:

- Bond fails due to the breaking up adhesive force between steel and concrete.
- Cushing concrete between steel ribs (Steel ribs are the lumps on the surface of steel bars that help the bars bond with concrete).
- Longitudinal splitting of concrete along reinforcement.

4.2.4 Factors to Increase Bond Strength

There are several factors by which we can increase the bond strength. If we can increase the bond strength, it will be beneficial for the structure. Some of the major factors are discussed as follows:

- The bar type has a lot of influence on bond strength. Instead of plain bars, bond strength increases if HYSD (High Yielding Strength Deformed Steel) bars are used.
- If the grade of concrete increases, then bond strength increases.
- Smaller diameter bars are provided instead of larger diameter bars in more numbers since the surface is for bond increases, so stress level decreases. Hence, strength increases.
- By providing more cover to reinforcement, bond strength can be increased.
- Bond strength can be enhanced by providing more shear reinforcement (i.e., stirrups). Another way to improve is to decrease the spacing of stirrups.
- Bond strength is improved by providing mechanical anchorages (bends & hooks).

4.2.5 Factors to Increase Bond Strength

There are several ways to provide anchorage in the beam:

By providing development length.

An extra bar, called development length, anchorage is provided inside the concrete. There was sufficient space below in the left-side figure of Fig.4.13 to provide development length, but in the right-side figure of Fig.4.13, there was insufficient space, so we just rounded the steel inside the beam. By rounding the bars inside the beam, we provided the required development length so that the beam would not fail in bond failure between steel and concrete. Thus, sufficient development lengths are ensured in the structural elements, and in any case, it should not be less than the required development length.

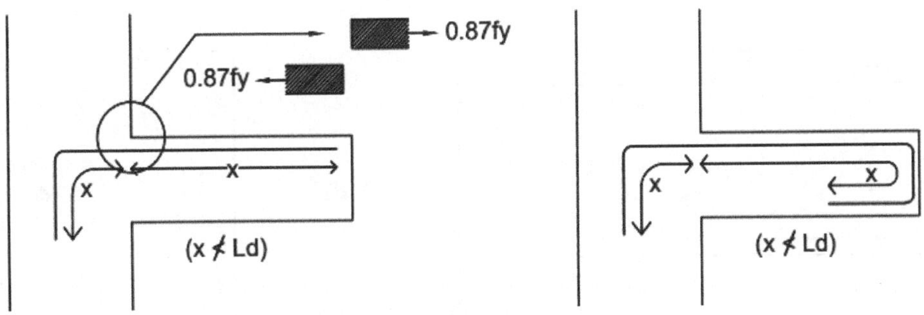

Figure 4.13: Provision of development length

By providing mechanical anchorage

Here, we are discussing mechanically providing anchorage (Fig.4.14). Physical fasteners, such as nails, dowels, bolts, and clamps, can deliver mechanical anchorages to structural elements.

One of the additional advantages of providing mechanical anchorage is that it eliminates the detailing problem that arises due to the joining of reinforcing bars.

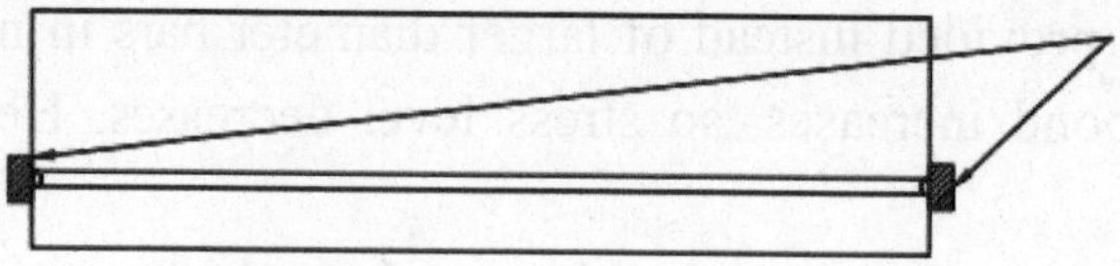

Figure 4.14: Provision of mechanical anchorage

By providing bends or hooks

Anchorage in bends or hooks is provided if sufficient development length cannot be provided inside the support due to insufficient space. For each 45° bend, an equivalent anchorage of 4φ is taken. The best for anchorage is 180° hook. Values of various standard bends are given in Table 4.4 as per Clause 4.3.1.2 of IS 456-2000

Table 4.4: Equivalent anchorage values

		Equivalent Acnhorage
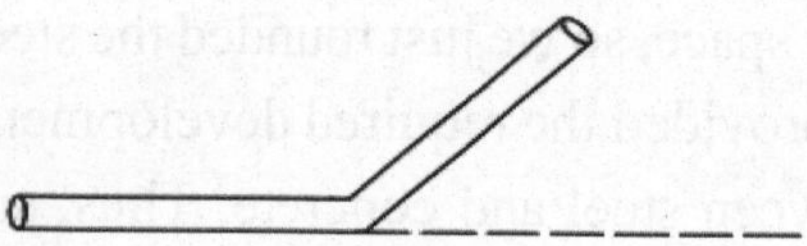	45°	4ϕ
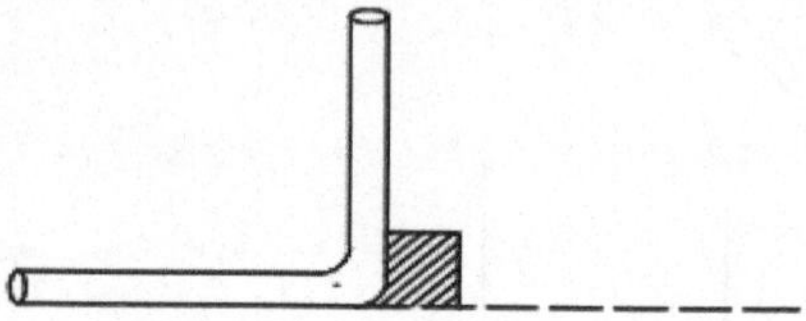	90°	8ϕ
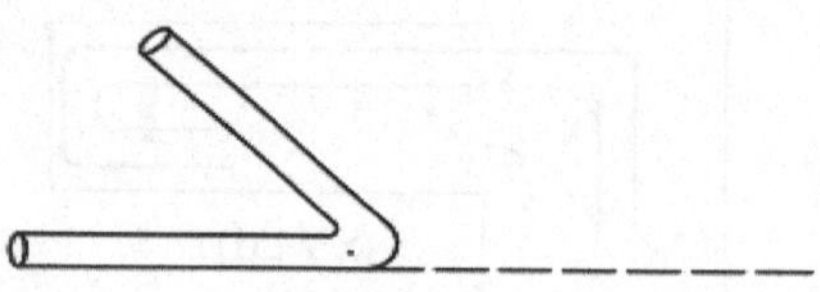	135°	12ϕ
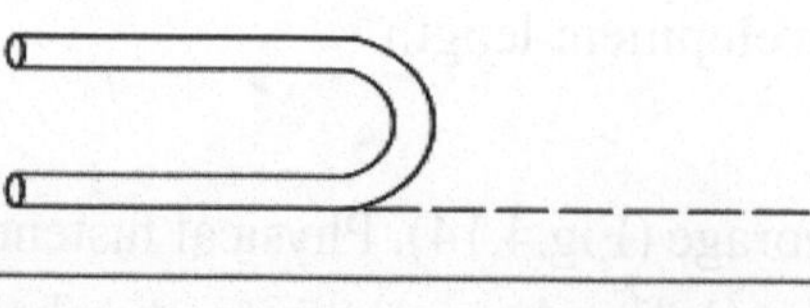	180°	16ϕ

Illustration 4.5 Determine the equivalent anchorage value for 135º bend for a bar of 8 mm dia.

Solution:

Equivalent anchorage (For 135º bend) = $12\varphi = 12 \times 8$ mm= 96 mm

4.3 LAPPING OF BARS

Lapping (Fig.4.15) is one of the essential works in reinforcement. Lapping can be defined as overlapping two bars side by side to get the desired length. Usually, the stock length of the steel bar is limited to 12 meters for ease of handling. But imagine there is a need to build a 100-foot-tall column, which is not practically available, and then multiple bars will be joined. The tension forces must be transferred from one bar to another at the location of discontinuity of the bar. So, the second bar is kept close to the first bar, and overlapping is done. The amount of overlap between two bars is called 'Lap length.' Lapping is generally done where bending stress is minimal, and all the bars of a particular column are not lapped at the same cross-section.

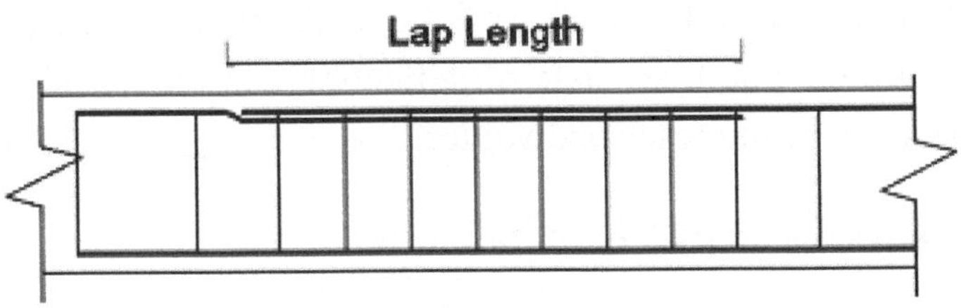

Figure 4.15: Lapping of bars

4.3.1 General Guidelines for Lapping as per IS 456-2000

- Lap splices shall not be used for bars larger than 32 mm in diameter; bars shall be welded or mechanically spliced for larger diameters.
- Lap length, including anchorage value of hooks in flexural tension, shall be equal to development length but not less than 30 times the diameter of the smaller bar.
- Lap length, including the anchorage value of hooks in direct tension, shall be equal to two times the development length but not less than 30 times the diameter of the smaller bar.

- Lap length in compression shall equal development length in compression but not less than 24 times the diameter of a smaller bar.

Illustration 4.6 The 20 mm diameter bar is proposed to be reduced to 16 mm in an axially loaded column. The grade of steel used is Fe 500. Determine the lap length if the design bond stress for M25 grade concrete is 1.4 MPa.

Solution:

In the compression zone, lap length is equal to development length in compression but not less than 24 times the diameter of a smaller bar.

Development length, $L_d = (0.87 f_y \varphi)/(4 T_{bd}) = (0.87 \times 500 \times 16) / (4 \times 1.25 \times 1.6 \times 1.4) = 621.43$ mm.

Now $24\varphi = 24 \times 16$ mm= 384 mm.

So, the lap length should be 621.43 mm.

4.3.2 Limit States of Serviceability

The limiting states of deflection and cracking in R.C. structures are some of the most important concepts to be taken care of. The limit state of deflection can be considered safe if the span-to-depth ratio of beams is within prescribed values.

4.3.3 Deflection Limits as per IS 456-2000

In an R.C. element, two main types of deflection are observed. The first is short-term deflections, and the second is long-term deflections.

Short-term deflections are due to elastic deformations immediately after the member is loaded. As time increases, deflections also keep increasing, mainly due to creep and shrinkage under sustained loads, and this deflection in aged elements is termed long-term deflection.

The deflection of a structure or part shall not adversely affect the appearance or efficiency of the structure finishes or partitions. As per Clause 23.2 of IS 456-2000 the deflection shall generally be limited to the following-

- Final deflections from cast level ≤ (Span/250)
- Final deflection due to partitions and finishes ≤ (Span/350) or 20 mm, whichever is less.

Short term deflections

This type of deflection is calculated by treating R.C. members as elastic members. In subjects like the strength of the material and structural analysis, the methods of finding deflections in beams are discussed elaborately.

Long term deflections

The main reasons behind long-term deflections are creep and shrinkage. Due to shrinkage, concrete tries to compress itself, but the reinforced steel gives tension to concrete to be in its original position, and alternatively, concrete applies compression to steel.

Creep is the continuous deflection of structural elements due to sustained loading. The modulus of elasticity of steel is also variable with time and dependent on creep.

Short-term modulus of elasticity of steel = $E = 5000\sqrt{f_{ck}}$

Long-term modulus of elasticity of steel = $E = (5000\sqrt{f_{ck}})/(1+\varphi)$, where φ is the creep coefficient.

Factors affecting deflection are-

- As the span length increases, deflection also increases.
- As the effective depth of span increases, deflection decreases.
- With the increase in percentage tensile reinforcement, deflection increases.
- If we also increase the percentage of bottom reinforcement, deflection decreases.

IS 456 also provides guidelines to keep the deflection of beams and slabs within safe limits so that the appearance and efficiency of the structure or partitions are not negatively affected.

Basic values of effective length to depth of different flexural members (beams, slabs, etc.) for spans up to 10 m as per Clause 23.2.1 of IS 456-2000 shall not exceed the following limits:

Type of member	*Effective length-to-depth ratio*
Cantilever	7
Simply Supported	20
Continuous	26

However, the above values depend on various factors based on different circumstances. The above standard values are multiplied by K_1, K_2, K_3, and K_4.

K_1= For spans exceeding 10 meters, this factor should be multiplied by the basic values.

= 10/Span

K_2= It depends on % tensile reinforcement. If % tensile reinforcement increases, deflection increases, so K_2 must be decreased.

K_3=It depends on % compression reinforcement. If % compression reinforcement increases, deflection decreases, so K_3 must be increased. If the beam is singly reinforced, take the K_3 value as 1.

K_4= It depends on the (b_w/b_f) ratio mainly used for I-beams. If b_w increases and deflection decreases, then K_4 must be increased.

Illustration 4.7 A cantilever beam of an effective length of 3.5 m has an effective depth of 400 mm. If K_1=1, K_2= 0.9, K_3= 1, K_4=1. Check if deflection criteria apply or not

Solution:

$L_{eff}/d < K_1 K_2 K_3 K_4$ (Basic value of effective length-to-span ratio for a cantilever beam)

$L_{eff}/d < 1 \times 0.9 \times 1 \times 1 \times 7 = 6.3$

Now $L_{eff}/d = 3500/400 = 8.75$

8.75 is not less than 6.3, so deflection is not under control.

Now, identify yourself with the options for controlling the deflection if they are not in the standard limits like in the above example.

4.3.4 Deflection Limits as per IS 456-2000

Some limits are specified as per Clause 23.3 of IS 456-2000 to ensure lateral stability in beams so that our structural element does not fail. These limits are-

- A supported or continuous beam shall be so proportionated that the clear distance between the lateral restraints does not exceed 60b or $250b^2/d$, whichever is less, where 'b' is the member's width and 'd' is the effective depth of the member.

- Similarly, for the cantilever beam, the clear distance between the lateral restraints does not exceed 25b or $100b^2/d$, whichever is less, where *'b'* is the member's width and *'d'* is the effective depth of the member.

SUMMARY

In RCC structures, shear forces are critical, especially in beams and slabs. High shear forces can lead to shear failure, so RCC elements are designed with adequate shear reinforcement. Another important aspect between concrete and steel is bond, which is essential for effective load transfer and overall structural performance. Poor bond results in slippage of bars, reducing the tensile strength of the structure and ultimately causing failure. Development length is important in providing a bond between steel and concrete without slippage or failure by transferring tensile forces. Determining and providing the development length is vital for RCC elements' structural integrity and safety.

EXERCISE

Make a few groups of students, each having 5 students. The students are assigned to design RCC beams for a small community hall that will serve as a multi-purpose space for 300 persons. The hall will host events like community meetings, indoor sports, and occasional small exhibitions.

- Calculate the shear force distribution along the beam's length.
- Identify the critical sections where shear force is maximum and needs to be addressed.
- Determine whether shear reinforcement (stirrups) is required at the critical sections.
- Design and propose the dimensions and spacing of the stirrups using IS 456:2000 guidelines.
- Calculate the development length for the main reinforcement bars in tension and compression zones.
- Identify potential modes of failure (diagonal tension, diagonal compression, or bond failure).

MULTIPLE CHOICE QUESTIONS

1. A reinforced concrete beam of a rectangular cross-section with a breadth of 230 mm and an effective depth of 400 mm is subjected to a maximum factored sheer force of 120 kN. The concrete, main steel, and stirrup steel grades are M20, Fe 415, and Fe 250,

respectively. For the area of the main steel provided, the design shear strength T_c as per IS 456-2000 is 0.48 N/mm^2. The beam is designed for a collapse limit state. The spacing of 2-legged 10 mm stirrups to be provided is (in mm):

A) 110

B) 107

C) 229

D) 180

2. In the design of reinforced concrete beams, if the requirement for the bond is not satisfied, the economical option to satisfy the requirement for the bond is to?

A) Provide smaller diameter bars more in number

B) Provide larger diameter bars less in number

C) Provide some additional mechanical anchorage devices in concrete

D) Bundling of bars

3. Punching shear failure is mainly seen in:

A) Cantilever beam

B) Thin slabs or footings

C) Propped cantilever beam

D) None of the above

4. The design shear strength of concrete for M20 grade of steel is:

A) 0.28

B) 0.62

C) 0.48

D) Any of the above options depends on the percentage of tensile steel

5. Flexural shear failure mainly occurs at

A) Where shear force is dominating

B) Where torsion is dominating

C) Where both bending moment and shear force are dominating

D) All of the above

6. When the spacing between shear reinforcement is decreased, bond strength-

A) Remains unchanged

B) Increases

C) May increase or decrease

D) Decrease

7. When HYSD bars are used instead of plain bars, the development length-

A) Can be increased

B) Can be decreased

C) It does not depend upon the type of bar

D) Can be reduced by 50%

8. A sufficient bond is required between steel and concrete for

A) The ease of casting of concrete

B) The ease of curing

C) For the ease of hydration reaction of cement

D) None of the above

9. As per IS 456-2000 for M20 grade concrete and plain bars in tension, the design bond stress is T_{bd}= 1.2 MPa. Further, IS 456-2000 permits this design bond stress value to be increased by 60% for HYSD bars. The stress in the HYSD reinforcing steel bars in tension is 360 MPa. Find the required development length, L_d, for HYSD bars in terms of the bar diameter, φ-

A) 34.54

B) 46.87

C) 89.25

D) 93.47

10. The reasons behind the bond between steel and concrete is-
    A) Adhesion between concrete and steel
    B) Frictional resistance between concrete and steel
    C) Mechanical resistance between steel and concrete
    D) All of the above

ANSWERS TO MULTIPLE CHOICE QUESTIONS

1	2	3	4	5	6	7
D	A	B	D	C	B	B
8	**9**	**10**				
D	B	D				

SHORT ANSWER TYPE QUESTIONS

1. What is shear stress in a reinforced concrete beam, and how is it calculated?
2. Explain why shear reinforcement is required in concrete beams.
3. What is the difference between nominal shear stress and design shear strength in concrete?
4. What is Punching shear failure? Write its significance in the concrete structure.
5. What is the role of bond stress in reinforced concrete structures?
6. Mention two factors that affect the bond between concrete and reinforcement bars.
7. How does the type of reinforcement (e.g., deformed vs. plain bars) influence bond strength?
8. Define development length and explain its importance in reinforced concrete.
9. Write the formula for calculating the development length of a reinforcing bar in concrete.

LONG ANSWER TYPE QUESTIONS

1. 5 no. of 16 mm diameter bars are provided as tensile reinforcement in the beam, out of which 2 no. of 16 mm diameter bars are bent up at 45°. The total factored shear force on the beam is 120 kN. The width of the beam is 230 mm, and the beam's effective depth is 460 mm. The grade of concrete and steel used is M20 and Fe 415. Design shear reinforcement for the beam considering a 6 mm diameter 2-legged vertical stirrup of grade Fe 250.
2. An RCC beam of rectangular cross-section has a factored shear force of 370 kN at its critical section. Its width is 250 mm, and its effective depth is 350 mm. Assume the design strength T_c of concrete is 0.62 N/mm^2 and the maximum allowable shear stress

T_c max is 2.8 N/mm^2. If two-legged 10 mm diameter vertical stirrups of Fe 250 grade steel are used, determine the required spacing (in cm, up to two decimal places) as per the limit state method.

3. Tie bars of 10 mm diameter will be provided in a concrete pavement slab. The working tensile stress of the tie bars is 230 MPa, the average bond strength between a tie bar and concrete is 2 MPa, and the joint gap between the slabs is 9 mm. Determine the design length of the tie bars in mm rounded off to the nearest integer.
4. If the design bond stress is 1.5 N/mm^2, determine the development length of a Fe 500 HYSD bar of nominal diameter 10 mm, fully stressed in tension.
5. If the angle of the bend is 45°, then the anchorage value of a hook is assumed to be many times the diameter of the bar.
6. Write down the factors that positively affect the bond strength between steel and concrete.
7. A cantilever beam of an effective length of 6 m has an effective depth of 400 mm. If K_1=1, K_2= 0.7, K_3= 1, K_4=1. Check if deflection criteria apply or not.
8. Write down the slenderness limits for the cantilever beam to ensure lateral stability.

TUTORIAL

Consider yourself a site engineer engaged in a project to construct a pedestrian bridge across a small canal. You are responsible for ensuring that the bridge beams' design considers shear pressures and that the steel and concrete are properly bonded for structural safety. Both foot loads and the occasional maintenance vehicle are applied to the bridge beams. You must evaluate how these loads affect the shear force in the beams, particularly near the supports.

KNOW MORE

For more information related to this topic, scan the QR code.

OR

Type this link in your browser

https://archive.nptel.ac.in/courses/105/105/105105104/

BIBLIOGRAPHY

1. Bureau of Indian Standards. (2000). IS 456:2000 - *Plain and Reinforced Concrete - Code of Practice* (4th Revision), New Delhi.
2. Duggal, S. K. (2014). *Reinforced Concrete Design*, Tata McGraw Hill Education: New Delhi.
3. Krishna Raju, and N. Pranesh, R.N. (2018). *Reinforced Concrete Design Principles and Practice*, New Age International: Mumbai.
4. Pillai, S.U., and Menon, D. (2017). *Reinforced Concrete Design*, McGraw Hill Publications: New Delhi.
5. Ramamrutham, S., & Narayanan, R. (2013). *Design of Reinforced Concrete Structures*, New Delhi: Dhanpat Rai Publishing Company.

5 DESIGN OF AXIALLY LOADED RCC COLUMN

UNIT SPECIFICS

In this unit, students will explore the fundamental concepts related to the design of columns, starting with their definition and classification based on the types of loads they carry. The unit introduces the limit state of compression members, focusing on the behaviour of columns under axial load and the factors that influence their strength and stability. The effective length of a column, which impacts its buckling behaviour, is also discussed in detail. The provisions of IS 456-2000 are outlined, including requirements for minimum and maximum steel reinforcement, cover, and tie spacing to ensure the column's structural integrity and safety. Students will then learn how to design axially loaded short columns, specifically square, rectangular, and circular columns, considering their dimensions, material properties, and loading conditions. Through practical examples, students will develop the skills to design safe and efficient compression members for real-world structural applications.

RATIONALE

The unit on the Design of Columns is crucial for providing students with a comprehensive understanding of the behaviour and design of compression members, which are integral to structural stability. As primary load-bearing components, columns must be designed to withstand axial loads without failure due to buckling or material failure. This unit introduces the classification of columns and the limit state of compression members, which ensures that columns perform within their safe limits under various load conditions. The concept of effective length is explored to understand how different column supports and boundary conditions influence buckling and overall stability. Provisions from IS 456-2000, such as minimum and maximum steel requirements, cover, and tie spacing, are essential for ensuring proper reinforcement and long-term durability of columns. Focusing on the design of axially loaded short columns that are square, rectangular, and circular, this unit equips students with the necessary skills to design safe, efficient compression members.

PRE-REQUISITE

Basic mathematics

UNIT OUTCOMES

The list of outcomes of this unit is as follows:

U5-O1: Introduction to RCC compression members

U5-O2: Understanding the effective length of columns

U5-O3: Design parameters for RCC columns

Unit Outcomes	Expected Mapping with Course Outcomes (1- Weak correlation; 2- Medium correlation; 3- Strong correlation)				
	CO-1	CO-2	CO-3	CO-4	CO-5
U5-O1	3	1	1	-	1
U5-O2	-	3	3	-	2
U5-O3	-	3	2	-	3

5.1 INTRODUCTION

A compression member is a structure component mainly pushed or squeezed rather than pulled or stretched by compressive pressures. These components are necessary for mechanical systems and structures because they resist compressive stress, which helps support loads. Occasionally, "column" and "compression member" are used interchangeably because the former is typical of all compression members. In other words, a structural element that experiences axial compressive forces is called a "compression member." As a component of the "vertical framing system," compression members are most frequently found in reinforced concrete buildings as columns (and occasionally as reinforced concrete walls). Rigid frame and truss members (sometimes called "struts") are other compression members. Clause 25.1.1 of IS 456-2000 defines the column as a compression member, the 'effective length' of which exceeds three times the least lateral dimension. Clause 26.5.3.1 (h) of IS 456-2000 defines 'pedestal' as a vertical compression member whose 'effective length' is less than three times its least lateral dimension.

5.2 CLASSIFICATION OF COLUMNS

Columns are categorised according to reinforcement, loading type, slenderness ratio, etc.

5.2.1 Classification of Columns Based on Type of Reinforcement

Depending on the kind of reinforcement used, columns made of reinforced concrete can be categorised into one of three categories:

- Spiral column: A continually coiled spiral reinforcement encircles the main longitudinal bars in close intervals.
- Tied Column: The main longitudinal bars are encased in lateral ties closely spaced apart.
- Composite columns: Structural steel sections (such as I-sections, channel sections, pipes, etc.) are used instead of primary reinforcing bars. Another way to put it would be that structural steel sections strengthen this column with or without longitudinal bars.

The two most popular types of columns used in reinforced concrete construction are spiral and tied columns, which are the main topics of this unit (Fig.5.1). Tied columns are more popular among the two since they may be used for any type of cross-sectional shape, including square, rectangular, T, L, and cross.

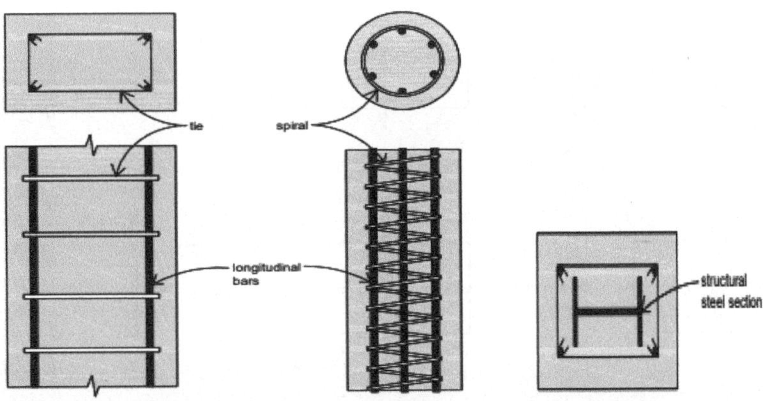

Figure 5.1: Tied, spiral, and composite columns.

5.2.2 Classification of Columns based on Type of Loading

Based on the type of loading (as shown in Fig.5.2), columns can be divided into the following three categories-

- Columns with axial loading: When considering the geometric centroidal axis of the column, the axial load acting on it is at zero eccentricity. However, pure axial cases are incredibly uncommon. Shear and possibly flexure are always present when a column experiences an axial load.
- Columns with uniaxial eccentric loading: In this case, the load's line of action is eccentric concerning one primary axis and zero concerning the other. Moments are generated concerning a single primary axis.
- Columns with biaxial eccentric loading: This one is the broadest kind of column. In this case, the two main axes of the column section are the eccentricity of the axial load's line of action. Moments are generated in two primary axes in this instance. If a column in a building is situated at one of the corners, its biaxial eccentricities are particularly important.

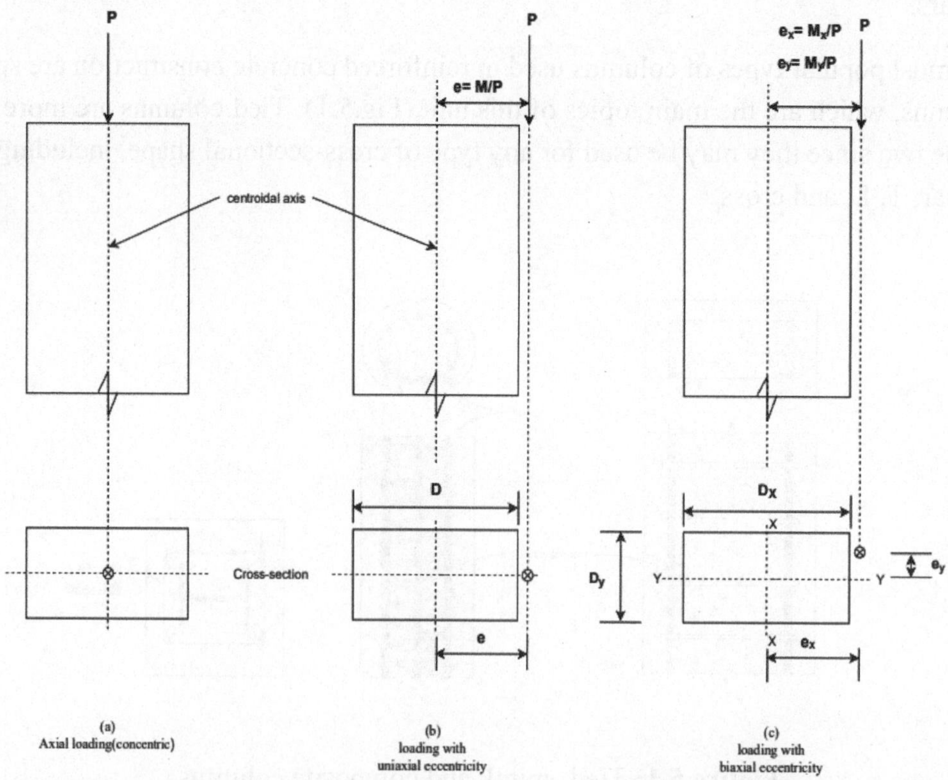

Figure 5.2: Different conditions of loading in column

Any column section that combines axial compression (*P*) and bending moment (*M*) is statically equivalent to a system where the load *P* is applied with an eccentricity of $e = M/P$ concerning the column section's longitudinal centroidal axis. More generally, in a loading scenario, the axially laden column has the simultaneous application of bending moments (M_x and M_y) about its major axis (XX) and minor axis (YY) in two perpendicular directions.

Columns with biaxial eccentricities, or those seen in reinforced concrete framed buildings, generally belong to the third type. Biaxial eccentricities are very important for the columns in the corners of buildings. These eccentricities under gravity loads are typically of a low order (about the lateral dimensions of the column) in the case of columns positioned inside symmetrical buildings. As a result, they are occasionally disregarded in design calculations. In these situations, it is considered that the columns belong to the first group, which is columns that have axial loading. However, IS 456-2000 ensures that these columns' designs are sufficiently conservative to withstand nominal aberrations in loading.

Often, one axis has little eccentricity, while there is much eccentricity about the other. Under such stresses, this condition arises in the external columns of the internal frames of a reinforced concrete structure.

All columns in multi-story buildings, whether internal or external, are susceptible to considerable uniaxial bending moments when subjected to lateral loads, whether seismic or wind-related. These columns belong to the second group, uniaxially eccentric columns.

5.2.3 Classification of Columns Based on Slenderness Ratio

Columns (i.e., compression members) can be categorised into one of two types based on the significance of slenderness effects:

- Short column
- Long/Slender column

The slenderness ratio is a geometrical property of the compression member associated with the column section. It is defined as the ratio of its 'effective length of column' to the lateral dimension of the column. This ratio, known as the "slenderness ratio," also indicates the column's sensitivity to elastic instability, or buckling, in the plane where the ratio is calculated. Low slenderness ratio columns short, stocky columns always break under ultimate loads when the material steel or concrete reaches its ultimate strength rather than buckling. Conversely, columns with extremely high slenderness ratios risk unexpectedly failing under relatively low compressive loads due to buckling, accompanied by a substantial lateral deflection.

A compression member may be categorised as a "short column" under Clause 25.1.2 of IS 456-2000 if its slenderness ratios about the "major principal axis" (l_{ex}/D_x) and the "minor principal axis" (l_{ey}/D_y) are both less than 12; if not, it should be treated as a "slender column." Here, l_{ex} and D_x stand for the effective length and lateral dimension (or "depth") for buckling in the plane that is normal to the major principal axis and passes through the longitudinal centroidal axis, causing buckling around the major axis. Similarly, l_{ey} and D_y are references to the minor principal axis.

$$\text{Slenderness ratio} = \frac{\textbf{Effective length of the column}}{\textbf{Least lateral cross-sectional dimension}}$$

However, in non-rectangular and non-circular sections, where the slenderness ratio is better defined in terms of the radius of gyration *(r)*, as in steel columns, rather than the lateral dimension *D*, such a definition is inappropriate.

Clauses 13.4, 13.5, and 13.6 of IS 456-2000 provide designs for short columns subjected to axial, uniaxially eccentric, and biaxially eccentric compression, respectively. Clause 13.3 explains the code's standards for minimum eccentricity, reinforcement, and slenderness limits. One crucial element in a column's design is its "effective length" (l_{ex}, l_{ey}). The following section describes techniques for estimating the effective length.

5.3 COLUMN EFFECTIVE LENGTH ESTIMATION

5.3.1 Definition of Effective Length

In each plane, the effective length of a column can be expressed as the distance between its points of inflexion while it is in its buckled state. The distance between lateral connections, or the actual length in the case of a cantilever, is known as the unsupported length *(l)*, and the boundary conditions at the column end introduced by connecting beams and other framing members determine the effective length. One can obtain an equation for l_e as:

$$l_e = kl$$

where k is the effective length ratio, also called the effective length factor, which is the ratio of the effective length to the unsupported length. The effective length factor's value is contingent upon the degree of translational and rotational restrictions at the column ends.

The "unsupported length" (*l*) of a column is clearly defined by Clause 25.1.3 of IS 456-2000 for various construction types. In a traditional framed building, it is assumed that the clear distance between the floor and the shallower beam framing into the columns in each direction at the next higher floor level. This implies that the unsupported length (buckling about a perpendicular axis) shall be assessed conservatively concerning the shallower beam when a column is framed in either direction by beams of differing depths on either side. It should be noted that the unsupported length may vary from the perpendicular direction in one direction. The terms $l_{ex} = k_x\, l_x$ and $l_{ey} = k_y\, l_y$ can be used to represent the effective lengths for buckling about the major and minor axes, respectively, for a rectangular column section (width $D_y \times$ depth D_x), where l_x and l_y stand for the corresponding unsupported lengths and k_x and k_y stands for the corresponding effective length factors. For more details about the unsupported length, refer to Clause 25.1.3 of IS 456-2000

5.3.2 Effective Length Ratios for Idealised Boundary Conditions

A frame is considered braced (against sideways) when relative transverse displacement between a column's upper and lower ends is prevented. In these situations, the effective length ratio (k) ranges from 0.5 to 1.0. A frame is considered unbraced (against sideway) when relative transverse displacement between a column's upper and lower ends is not prevented. The effective length ratio (k) in these situations ranges from 1.0 to infinity.

While it may be advantageous in design practice to assume idealised boundary conditions at a column end, such as zero or full restriction (both translational and rotational), the reality is that actual constructions typically cannot realise such idealisations. Clause E–1 of IS 456-2000 permits these idealisations but advises using "effective length ratios" ($k = l_e/l$), which are typically more conservative than those derived from theoretical considerations. To get the value of 'k,' one can refer to Annexure.

5.4 THE CODAL RECOMMENDATIONS OF IS 456:2000 FOR THE DESIGN OF COLUMNS

5.4.1 Slenderness Ratio

Since more "secondary" moments are introduced due to slenderness effects in columns, strength is effectively reduced. When it comes to extremely thin columns, instability (also known as "elastic buckling"), as opposed to material failure, can cause failure rapidly under light loads. IS 456-2000 aims to stop this instability-related failure by defining specific "slenderness limits" in the column proportioning. The slenderness of a column subjected to extreme compression has a significant consequence. The impact of the axial compression in the displaced geometry of the column creates "secondary moments" when a column experiences both flexure and axial compression.

Clause 25.3.1 of IS 456-2000 recommends that the unsupported length between end restraints cannot exceed 60 times a column's least lateral dimension.

$$\frac{l}{d} \leq 60$$

Moreover, Clause 25.3.2 of IS 456-2000 states that if a column has a free end (a cantilevered column) in any given plane, its unsupported length 'L', should not exceed $100b^2/D$

$$\text{i.e.,} \quad L \leq \frac{100b^2}{D}$$

where D is the depth of the cross-section measured in the plane of the cantilever and b is the width (in the perpendicular direction).

5.4.2 Minimum Eccentricities

A general loading situation on a compression member combines biaxial bending with axial compression, as discussed in a prior section. This loading condition is represented by a biaxial eccentric compression state, in which the major and minor primary axes have eccentricities e_x and e_y, respectively, and the axial load P acts eccentric to the longitudinal centroidal axis of the column cross-section.

Frequently, eccentricities that are not directly derived from structural analysis computations affect the column for several reasons, including:

- lateral loads not considered during design;
- live load locations not considered during design;
- inadvertent lateral or eccentric loads;
- construction errors (e.g., misalignments); and
- underestimated slenderness effects during design.

Therefore, to encounter these problems, Clause 25.4 of IS 456-2000 suggests that every column be designed for a minimum eccentricity e_{min} (in any plane) equal to the unsupported length/500 plus lateral dimension/30, subject to a minimum of 20 mm.

This suggests the following for a column with a rectangular section (Fig.5.2), the minimum eccentricity along the x-direction will be-

$$e_{x,min} = \begin{Bmatrix} \frac{l}{500} + \frac{Dx}{30} \\ 20mm \end{Bmatrix} \text{ whichever is maximum.}$$

Similarly, the minimum eccentricity along the y-direction shall be calculated.

5.4.3 Reinforcement and its Detailing

Longitudinal reinforcement (Clause 26.5.3.1 of IS 456-2000)

Generally, the cross-sectional area of the longitudinal bars must be at least 0.8 percent of the gross area of the column section (Fig.5.3). IS 456-2000 stipulates these minimal limits to provide nominal flexural resistance in the event of unanticipated loading eccentricity and to prevent the bars from yielding due to shrinkage and creep, which causes the load to shift from the concrete to their reinforcement.

When axial compression is applied to particularly big columns (where the size is determined, for example, by architectural reasons rather than strength), the restriction of 0.8 percent of the gross area may lead to excessive reinforcement. IS 456-2000 makes an exception in these situations by allowing the minimum area of steel to be determined as 0.8 percent of the area of concrete needed to withstand the direct stress rather than the actual (gross) area.

Nonetheless, 0.15 percent of the gross area of the cross-section may be considered the minimum need for longitudinal bars in the case of pedestals (i.e., compression members with $l_e/D < 3$) that are intended as simple concrete columns. Clause 32.5 of IS 456-2000 has added specific standards for the minimum vertical (and horizontal) steel reinforcement for reinforced concrete walls. Vertical reinforcement should generally comprise at least 0.15 percent of the gross area. If deformed bars (Fe 415/Fe 500 grade steel) or welded wire cloth are used, this could be lowered to 0.12% if the bar diameter is less than 16 mm. The wall should have two layers of this reinforcement if it is thicker than 200 mm. Bar spacing should always be no more than 450 mm, or three times the thickness of the wall, whichever is less.

- It is recommended that the longitudinal bars' necessary cross-sectional area not exceed 6% of the gross area of the column section. However, a lower upper limit of 4% is generally advised to improve concrete placing and compaction, especially at lapped splice places. Columns on the lowest floors of tall buildings typically have much reinforcement (about 4%). At higher levels, the bars are gradually reduced in phases.

- Columns (and pedestals) should have longitudinal bars that are at least 12 mm in diameter and no more than 300 mm apart (centre-to-centre) along the column's edge. A rectangular column should have at least four bars (one at each corner); in a circular column, at least six bars are equally spaced around the perimeter. The longitudinal bars in "spiral columns, including noncircular ones, should be positioned equally around the inner circumference of the spiral reinforcement and in contact with it. There should be at least one bar at each corner or apex of columns with T, L, or other cross-sectional configurations. Although longitudinal bars are often positioned at the column's edge (for improved flexural resistance), they can also be positioned inside when loading eccentricities are low. When many bars must fit together, they might be bundled or, on the other hand, clustered.
- Clause 26.4.2.1 of IS 456-2000 recommends a minimum clear cover of 40 mm or bar diameter (whichever is greater) to the column ties for columns in general; small-sized columns *(D* $\leq$ 200 mm and whose reinforcing bars do not exceed 12 mm) may have a reduced clear cover of 25 mm, and walls must have a minimum clear cover of 15 mm (or bar diameter, whichever is greater). Providing more cover in harsh circumstances is desirable, but ideally no more than 75 mm, for durability's sake.

Transverse reinforcement

To improve the column's resistance to bending and avoid buckling or failure under load, supplementary reinforcement is used to withstand lateral or transverse stresses, such as those caused by shear and torsion. Clause 26.5.3.2 of IS 456-2000 recommends that all longitudinal reinforcement in a compression member should be enclosed within transverse reinforcement, which can be lateral ties with internal angles not greater than 135 degrees or spirals. Tie bars are necessarily provided in columns for keeping the longitudinal bars in place during construction, restricting the concrete in the core, which eventually improves ductility and strength and avoids the early buckling of individual bars.

Lateral Ties

How lateral ties are arranged should effectively meet the aforementioned standards. They should give each longitudinal bar enough lateral support to prevent it from moving outward. The diameter of the tie ϕ_t is not affected by the quality of steel because stiffness needs rather than strength requirements determine it. The ties' pitch s_t (the distance between the centres along the column's longitudinal axis) should be sufficiently small to lower each longitudinal bar's unsupported length and slenderness ratio. The IS 456-2000 recommends the diameter and spacing of the ties (i.e., pitch) as follows:

$$\text{Tie diameter } (\phi_t) \geq \begin{cases} \text{Diameter of main bar}/4 \\ 6\text{mm} \end{cases}$$

$$\text{Spacing of tie, pitch } (s_t) \leq \begin{cases} 16 \times \text{Diameter of smaller diameter of main bar} \\ \text{Least lateral dimension of the column } (D) \\ 300 \text{ mm} \end{cases}$$

where D represents the column's least lateral dimension.

Every longitudinal bar the tie encloses, especially the corner bars, should ideally be completely lateral restrained by the tie turning around. Only the corner and alternating bars require lateral support when the longitudinal bar spacing is less than 75 mm. When the concrete core is compressed, the straight section of a closed tie (between the corner bars) tends to bulge outward, making it ineffective if it is very large. Therefore, more cross-connections are necessary for the concrete to be effectively contained. When the longitudinal bars separated by less than $48\varphi_t$ are successfully connected in two directions, the extra longitudinal bars between them only need to be tied in one direction using open ties. Every tie, whether open or closed, must have its ends securely fastened. Each group of longitudinal bars should be tied separately when arranged at the corners of a large column. Additionally, all groups should be tied together with a single closed tie. Multiple ties in columns should be staggered along the longitudinal axis, with extra ties provided at lapped splice locations, especially at bends.

Spirals

Helical reinforcement greatly improves the column's ductility under ultimate loads and offers excellent confinement to the concrete in the "core." The spiral's pitch and diameter can be calculated similarly to ties, except when the column is intended to support a 5% overload as IS 456-2000 allows. In this case, the pitch of the spiral ties should be as follows:

$$\text{Maximum spacing of spiral tie, } \textbf{pitch } (s_t) < \begin{cases} \text{Core diameter}/6 \\ 75\text{mm} \end{cases}$$

$$\text{Minimum spacing of spiral ties, } \textbf{pitch } (s_t) > \begin{cases} 25 \text{ mm} \\ 3 \text{ times the diameter of tie} \end{cases}$$

The spiral's ends should have an additional 1.5 revolutions to ensure adequate anchoring.

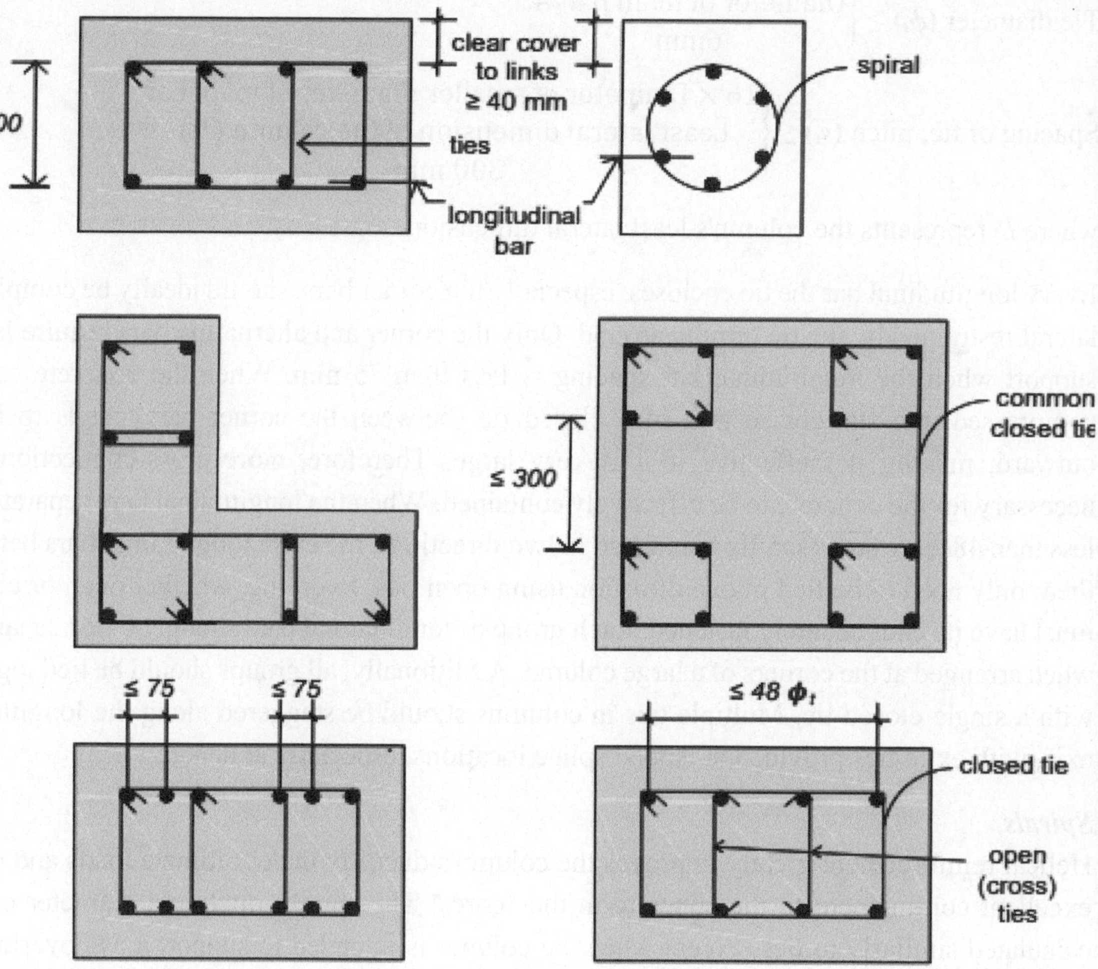

Figure 5.3: IS 456-2000 recommendations for reinforcement detailing in column

Illustration 5.1 A rectangular RC column of 400 mm × 600 mm with an effective length of 3.5 m is provided, with both ends rotationally free and braced against side sway; determine the slenderness ratios and comment about the column type.

Solution:

To check the column as short or long,

$$\text{Slenderness ratio} = \frac{\text{Effective length of the column}}{\text{Least lateral cross-sectional dimension}}$$

Effective length of column (l_e) = l_{ex} = l_{ey} = 3500 mm

Least lateral dimension along x-direction (D_x) = 400 mm

Least lateral dimension along y-direction (D_y) = 600 mm

Therefore, Slenderness ratio along Y-direction (λ_x) = l_{ex}/D_x = 3500/400 = 8.75 < 12

Slenderness ratio along Y-direction (λ_y) = l_{ey}/D_y = 3500/600 = 5.83 < 12

Thus, the slenderness ratio in both directions is less than 12, so the column is categorised as a short column.

Illustration 5.2 Calculate the minimum eccentricities for the column given in Illustration 5.1.

Solution:
For a column that has both the ends rotationally free and braced against side sway, effective length ratio k=1,

So, the unsupported length = effective length of the column

=> $l_x = l_{ex}$ and $l_y = l_{ey}$

Eccentricity is given as, $e = \begin{Bmatrix} \frac{l}{500} + \frac{D}{30} \\ 20\text{mm} \end{Bmatrix}$ whichever is maximum

$$e_{x,min} = \begin{Bmatrix} \frac{lex}{500} + \frac{Dx}{30} \\ 20\text{mm} \end{Bmatrix} \text{ whichever is maximum}$$

$$= \begin{Bmatrix} \frac{3500}{500} + \frac{400}{30} \\ 20\text{mm} \end{Bmatrix} \max = \begin{Bmatrix} 20.33\text{mm} \\ 20\text{mm} \end{Bmatrix} \max = 20.33 \text{ mm}$$

$$e_{y,min} = \begin{Bmatrix} \frac{ley}{500} + \frac{Dy}{30} \\ 20\text{mm} \end{Bmatrix} \text{ whichever is maximum}$$

$$= \begin{Bmatrix} \frac{3500}{500} + \frac{600}{30} \\ 20\text{mm} \end{Bmatrix} \max = \begin{Bmatrix} 27\text{mm} \\ 20\text{mm} \end{Bmatrix} \max = 27 \text{ mm}$$

5.5 DESIGN OF SHORT COLUMN UNDER AXIAL COMPRESSION

5.5.1 Axial Loading Conditions

A compression member is said to be subjected to axial loading if the loading results in a homogeneous distribution of compressive strain throughout the cross-section. The line of action of the load P_o must align with the longitudinal centroidal axis of the column section if the column is symmetrically reinforced to generate a uniform strain distribution. The section's resulting compressive force, C_c+C_s, must act through the external load at the point of application of P_o and be equal to it for there to be equilibrium. If f_{cc} and f_{sc} represent the longitudinal steel and concrete stresses, respectively, they correspond to the uniform compressive strain ε_c. So, we can write it as:

$$P_o = C_c + C_o$$

$$= f_{cc}A_c + f_{sc}A_{sc}$$

$$\text{Therefore, } P_o = f_{cc}A_g + (f_{sc} - f_{cc})\, A_{sc}$$

In the above equation,

A_g = Gross area of cross-section = $A_c + A_{sc}$

A_{sc} = Total area of longitudinal reinforcement

A_c = Net area of concrete in the section = $A_g - A_{sc}$

5.5.2 Columns under Service Load

Elastic theory, which includes permissible stresses, modular ratio, and transformed section, was used to design reinforced concrete columns until the early 1950s. Afterwards, it was discovered through considerable experimental research that, even in the case of axial loading, there can never be a constant ratio of steel stress f_{sc} to concrete stress f_{cc}. The ratio of these stresses was determined by:

- The history of continuous loading and several concrete quality-related parameters impact the degree of creep.
- The concrete's age, curing technique, environmental factors, and other quality-related issues influenced how much shrinkage occurred.

The strain in the cross-section ε_c generally increases with age due to creep and shrinkage. This causes the strains in steel and concrete to redistribute, transferring some of the load that the steel and concrete share. As a result, it becomes challenging to forecast the f_{cc} and f_{sc} stresses under service loads. By the standard working stress method of design, the acceptable stresses σ_{cc} and σ_{sc} are substituted for f_{sc} and f_{cc}, respectively.

Therefore, as per the working stress method of design, the design equation can be given as

$$P_o = \sigma_{cc} A_g + (\sigma_{cc} - \sigma_{sc}) A_{sc}$$

where σ_{sc} is roughly set at 1.5m σ_{cc}. This assumption, however, produces unrealistic and unfeasible designs by making the steel stress σ_{sc} independent of the steel grade. As per Clause B 2.2 of IS 456-2000 a working stress design is recommended to address this issue.

Table 5.1: The allowable stresses in steel (σ_{sc}) under direct compression

Steel	σ_{sc}
Fe 250	130 MPa
Fe 415, Fe 500	190 MPa

Table 5.2: The allowable stresses in concrete (σ_{cc}) under direct compression

Grade of Concrete	**Allowable stresses in concrete (σ_{cc})**
M15	4.0 MPa
M20	5.0 MPa
M25	6.0 MPa
M30	8.0 MPa
M35	9.0 MPa

Other countries' codes have replaced the working stress method (WSM) with the ultimate load method (ULM) and, later, the rational limit states method (LSM).

5.5.3 Column under Ultimate Loads

Under ultimate load conditions, an axially compressed short column behaves in a somewhat predictable manner, in contrast to service load situations. The column's final strength is determined to be mostly unaffected by its age and loading history. The column's axial shortening grows linearly with increasing axial loading, reaching roughly 80% of the ultimate load P_{uo}.

It has been discovered that this behaviour is unaffected by transverse reinforcement. However, the behaviour is dependent on the kind and quantity of transverse reinforcement after the ultimate load (point B in Fig.5.4)

Tied columns

The longitudinal steel would generally have reached "yield" conditions at the ultimate load level P_{uo} (point B in Fig.5.4), regardless of the presence or absence of transverse reinforcing. With widely separated lateral ties or without transverse reinforcement, the longitudinal bars will buckle, and the concrete will compress and shear, leading to a quick and brittle failure. With closely spaced lateral ties that give under tension before the columns collapse, some marginal ductility (Paths BC, BD in Fig.5.4) can be added to linked columns. The concrete's "softening" and microcracking are the reasons for the load-axial shortening curve's decline.

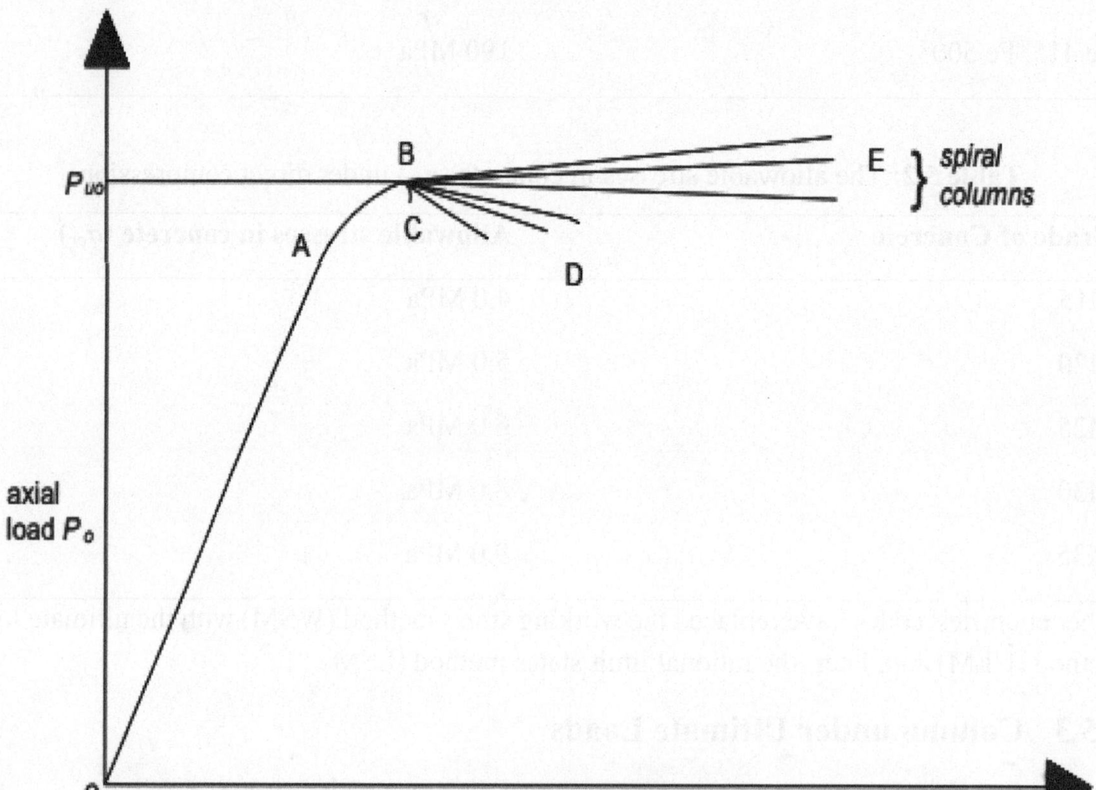

Figure 5.4: Behaviour of axially loaded tied and spiral columns

Spiral columns

In the spiral column, significant ductility is attained before the column collapses (BE in Fig. 5.4). The exterior shell of the concrete, which covers the spiral, is observed to spall off about load level P_{uo} (Point B in Fig.5.4). However, the concrete in the "core," laterally constrained by the helical reinforcement, continues to support the load. Collapse eventually occurs when the spiral reinforcement gives way under stress. If there is enough spiral reinforcement, the load-bearing capacity after spalling can surpass P_{uo}, more than compensating for the load capacity lost because of the concrete shell's spalling. Based on this Clause 39.4 of IS 456-2000 allows the increase of the column's load-carrying capacity by 5% beyond the ultimate load, assuming the following criteria are fulfilled:

$$\frac{\text{Volume of spiral reinforcement per unit length}}{\text{Volume of core}} \geq 0.36\left(\frac{fc}{fy}\right)\left(\frac{Ag}{Ac}-1\right)$$

where, A_g = gross area of the cross-section $= \frac{\pi}{4}(D_g)^2$

D_g = gross diameter

A_c = core area of concrete $= \frac{\pi}{4}(D_c)^2$

D_c = Core diameter

Core volume for unit length (i.e., 1m= 1000mm)

$V_c = 1000A_c$

V_h = Volume of helical reinforcement for the same unit length

V_h = (Number of turns) × (length of one turn) × (cross-sectional area of helical reinforcement)

D_h = Diameter of helical reinforcement $= D_c - \phi_h$

Now, length of helix in one turn $= \sqrt{(\pi D_h)^2 + p^2} \approx \pi D_h$

Therefore, the volume of helical reinforcement in 1000 mm can be determined by:

$V_h = (1000/p) \times (\pi D_h) \times \frac{\pi}{4}\phi_h^2$

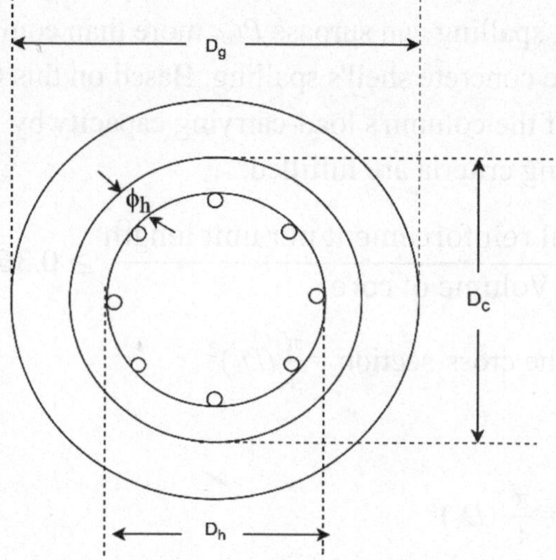

Figure 5.5: Cross-section of a spiral column

5.5.4 Design Strength of Axially Loaded Short Columns

Clause 39.1a of IS 456-2000, specifies $\varepsilon_c = 0.002$ as the maximum compressive strain in concrete under axial loading at the limit state of collapse in compression. According to this (quite cautious) limiting strain of 0.002, the design stress in steel is $0.87f_y$ in the case of Fe 250 and $0.790f_y$ and $0.746f_y$ in the cases of Fe 415 and Fe 500, respectively, and the design stress in concrete is $0.67f_{ck}/1.5 = 0.447f_{ck}$. So, the design strength of a short column under pure axial loading is given as follows:

$$P_{uo} = 0.447\, f_{ck}\, A_g + (f_{sc} - 0.447 f_{ck})\, A_{sc}$$

where,

$$f_{sc} = \begin{cases} 0.87fy \text{ for Fe 250} \\ 0.79fy \text{ for Fe 415} \\ 0.746fy \text{ for Fe 500} \end{cases}$$

However, as discussed earlier, IS 456-2000 mandates that all columns be built for "minimum eccentricities" when loading. Thus, it is not possible to apply the previous equation directly. Nevertheless, Clause 39.3 of IS 456-2000 allows using the following simplified formula, derived by lowering P_{uo} by roughly 10% in cases where the estimated minimum eccentricity (in any plane) does not exceed 0.05 times the lateral dimension (in the plane examined).

$$P_{uo} = 0.4\, f_{ck} A_g + (0.67 f_y - 0.47 f_{ck})\, A_{sc}$$

P_{uo} stands for the design strength in uniaxial compression that IS 456-2000 allows, considering the effect of the minimum eccentricities. When the equation is applied, a conservative design is produced instead of a rigorous design incorporating axial compression and biaxial bending with the minimum eccentricities. As previously stated, Clause 39.4 of IS 456-2000 allows for a 5% increase in load capacity when spiral reinforcement is used.

Illustration 5.3 An RC short column of 450 mm × 450 mm is reinforced with 4 no. of 20 mm diameter bars of grade Fe 415. Find the concentric working load-carrying capacity of a column by ignoring eccentricity. Use M20 grade of concrete.

Solution:

Gross area of column= (450x450) mm^2

Ultimate load carrying capacity of column, $P_u = 0.45 f_{ck} A_c + 0.75 f_y A_{sc}$

Where f_{ck} = Characteristics compressive strength of concrete,

A_c= Area of concrete portion,

f_y= Yield strength of steel,

A_{sc} = Area of steel in concrete.

$P_{ul} = 0.45 \times 20 \times [450^2 - 4 \times (\pi/4) \times 20^2] + 0.75415 \times 4 \times (\pi/4) \times 20^2$

=2202.318 kN

So, the working load carrying capacity of the column = $P_u/1.5$ = 1468.212 kN.

Illustration 5.4 Calculate the axial load carrying capacity of a column section 500 mm x 600 mm in section, reinforced with 8 no. of 20 mm diameter bars of grade Fe 415. Use M20 grade of concrete.

Solution:

Ultimate axial load carrying capacity of column = $(0.4 \times 20 \times 500 \times 600) + [\{(0.67 \times 415) - (0.4 \times 20)\} \times 8 \times (\pi/4) \times 20^2]$

= 3078.8 kN.

Illustration 5.5 Design a reinforced concrete column (450 x 600) mm in size subjected to an axial load of 2000 kN under service load conditions. The unsupported length of the column is 3 meters. The grade of steel used is Fe 415, and the grade of concrete is M20. Both the ends of the column are pinned.

Solution:

The first step is to check whether it is a short column. So, we need to check the slenderness ratio. Since both the ends of the column are pinned, the unsupported length is 3 meters or 3000 mm.

Slenderness ratio = L/b = 3000/450 = 6.67

3 < 6.67 < 12, so it is a short column.

The next step is to check for minimum eccentricity,

$e_{min,x}$ is the maximum among the following:

i) L_{un} / 500 + D/30 = (3000/500) + (600/30) = 26 mm

ii) 20 mm

So, the maximum eccentricity along the x direction is 26 mm.

$e_{min,y}$ is the maximum among the following:

i) L_{un} / 500 + b / 30 = (3000/500) + (450/30) = 21 mm.

ii) 20 mm.

So, the maximum eccentricity along the y direction is 21 mm.

$e_{min,x} < 0.05D = 26 \text{ mm} < 0.05 \times 600 = 30 \text{ mm}$.

$e_{min,y} < 0.05b = 21 \text{ mm} < 0.05 \times 450 = 22.5 \text{ mm}$.

The next step is to find the area of steel in compression.

$P_u = 0.4 f_{ck} A_g + (0.67 f_y - 0.4 f_{ck}) A_{sc}$

$P_u = 1.5 \times 2000 = 3000\text{kN}$.

$3000 \times 10^3 = 0.4 \times 20 \times 450 \times 600 + \{(0.67 \times 415) - (0.4 \times 20)\} A_{sc}$

$A_{sc} = 3110.5 \text{ mm}^2$

So, provide 4 no. of 20 mm φ and 4 no. of 25 mm φ.

So, the area of steel provided is 3220.5 mm^2.

Also, let us check the minimum area of steel requirement.

$A_{sc,\,min}$ = 0.8% of gross area = 0.8% of (450 × 600) = 2160 mm^2.

So $A_{sc,\ min} < A_{sc,\ provided}$. Hence ok.

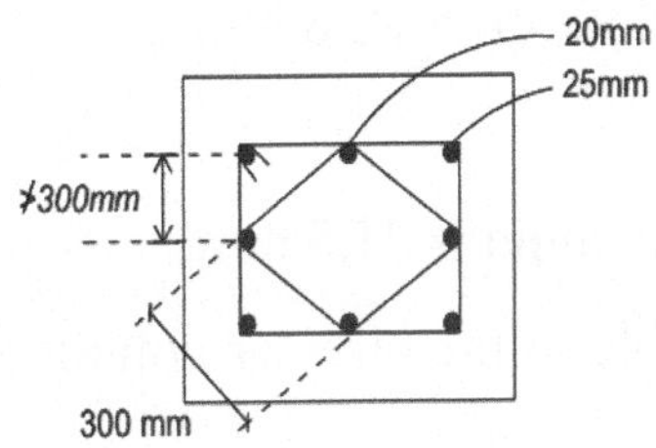

Figure 5.6: Reinforcement detailing

Illustration 5.6 In Illustration 5.5, provide lateral ties as per IS 456-2000 specifications.

Solution:

As per IS 456-2000, the diameter of lateral ties should be larger than the maximum among the following-

i) $\varphi_{longitudinal,\ max}/4 = 6.25$ mm.

ii) 6 mm.

So, 8 mm diameter bars should be provided as lateral reinforcement.

As per IS 456-2000, the spacing of lateral ties should be smaller than the minimum among the following-

i) Least lateral dimension 450 mm.

ii) 300 mm.

iii) $16\varphi_{longitudinal,\ min} = 16 \times 20 = 320$ mm.

So, provide spacing of 300 mm.

As lateral reinforcement, 8 mm diameter bars are provided at 300 mm centre to centre.

Illustration 5.7 Check whether the circular column with a diameter of 450 mm is axially loaded. The unsupported length of the column is 3.4 meters, and both ends are pin-supported. The factored axial load on the column is 7000 kN.

Solution:

e_{min} is the maximum among the following-

i) $L_{un}/500 + D/30 = (3400/500) + (450/30) = 21.8$ mm.

ii) 20 mm

So, the eccentricity of the circular column is 21.8 mm.

Maximum eccentricity is permissible in the circular column= 0.05D= 0.05 × 450 mm= 22.5 mm.

So, $e_{min,x} < 0.05D$. Hence, the circular column is axially loaded.

Illustration 5.8 Calculate the dimensions of a rectangular column subjected to a factored axial load of 4000 kN. The unsupported length of the column is 3.4 m, and the column is pin-jointed at both ends. Use Fe 415 grade of steel and M20 grade of concrete. Assume the percentage of steel as 1.5% of the gross area of the column.

Solution:

It is given to take steel as 1.5% of the gross area of steel.

Let us assume $D/b = 1.25$

$4000 \times 10^3 = 0.4 \times 20 \times A_g + \{(0.67 \times 415) - (0.4 \times 20)\}$ (1.5% of A_g)

$A_g = 331929.54$ mm².

$Db = 331929.54$ mm²

$(1.25\ b) = 331929.54$ mm²

$b = 515.30$ mm.

Let us provide 520 mm.

So, $D = 1.25b = 1.25 \times 520 = 650$ mm.

So, the dimension of the rectangular column becomes (520 × 650) mm.

And area of steel provided= 1.5 of (520 × 650) = 5070 mm².

Illustration 5.9 Design a short circular column subjected to an axial load of 1200 kN under service load conditions using M30 grade concrete and Fe 415 grade steel. The column is to be provided with spiral ties.

Solution:

For short column load carrying capacity is given by:

$P_u = 0.4\, f_{ck}\, A_g + (0.67 f_y - 0.40 f_{ck})\, A_{sc}$

Axial load given (P) = 1200 kN

Factored axial load (P_u) =1.5 × 1200 = 1800kN

So, for the preliminary design, let us take the percentage of steel to be provided as 1.2% (greater than the minimum requirement of 0.8%).

Thus, $A_{sc} = 0.012\, A_g$

Therefore, $P_u = 0.4\, f_{ck}\, A_g + (0.67 f_y - 0.40 f_{ck})\, A_{sc}$

$1800 \times 10^3 = 0.4 \times 30 \times A_g + (0.67 \times 415 - 0.40 \times 30)\, 0.012 \times A_g$

$\Rightarrow 1800 \times 10^3 = 15.193 \times A_g$

$A_g = 118.48 \times 10^3\ \text{mm}^2$

$\Rightarrow (\pi/4) \times D^2 = 118.48 \times 10^3\ \text{mm}^2$

$\Rightarrow D = 388.396$ mm

So, provide $D = 400$ mm

So, $A_{g,\,provided} = 125663.71\ \text{mm}^2 > 118.48 \times 10^3\ \text{mm}^2$. (OK)

Now, Area of steel reinforcement, $A_{sc} = 0.012\, A_g = 0.012 \times (\pi/4) \times 400^2 = 1507.96\ \text{mm}^2$

As we have to provide spiral ties, a minimum 6 number of bars are to be provided.

Therefore, using 8-16 mm diameter bars,

$A_{sc\ provided} = 8 \times (\pi/4) \times 16^2 = 1608.50\ \text{mm}^2 > 1507.96\ \text{mm}^2$ (OK)

Provide 8-16 mm diameter bars at equal spacing on the periphery of the circular column.

Provision of spiral reinforcement

The minimum clear cover requirement for a column is 40 mm.

Assuming a clear cover of 45 mm, the diameter of the core of the column will be,

$D_c = 400 - (2 \times 45) = 310$mm

The minimum diameter of the spiral, as per IS 456:2000, is 6mm.

So, using 6 mm diameter spirals at a pitch of 's_t.'

Therefore, for spiral reinforcement,

$$\frac{\text{Volume of spiral reinforcement per unit length}}{\text{Volume of core}} \geq 0.36\left(\frac{\text{fck}}{\text{fy}}\right)\left(\frac{\text{Ag}}{\text{Acore}} - 1\right)$$

Where,

$$\frac{\text{Volume of spiral reinforcement per unit length}}{\text{Volume of core}} = \frac{\left(\frac{\pi}{4}\right) \times 6^2 \times \pi \times (310 - 6)/\text{st}}{\left(\frac{\pi}{4}\right) \times 310^2}$$

$$= 0.3578 / \text{s}_\text{t}$$

$$0.36\left(\frac{\text{fck}}{\text{fy}}\right)\left(\frac{\text{Ag}}{\text{Acore}} - 1\right) = 0.36 \times \left(\frac{30}{415}\right) \times \left(\frac{(\pi/4) \times 400^2}{(\pi/4) \times 310^2} - 1\right)$$

$= 0.0173$

Now, $0.3578 / s_t \geq 0.0173$

$s_t \leq 20.682$ mm

As per IS 456:2000,

Maximum spacing of spiral tie, pitch $(s_t) < \begin{cases} \text{Core diameter}/6 \\ 75\text{mm} \end{cases}$

$(s_t) < \begin{cases} \frac{310}{6} = 51.67 \text{ mm} \\ 75\text{mm} \end{cases} = 51.67$ mm

Minimum spacing of spiral ties, pitch $(s_t) > \begin{cases} 25 \text{ mm} \\ 3 \text{ times the diameter of tie} \end{cases}$

$(s_t) > \begin{cases} 25 \text{ mm} \\ 3 \times 6 = 18 \text{ mm} \end{cases} = 25$ mm

Thus, provide 6 mm spiral ties @ pitch of 30 mm c/c. (≥ 25 mm and < 51.67 mm)

Reinforcement detailing

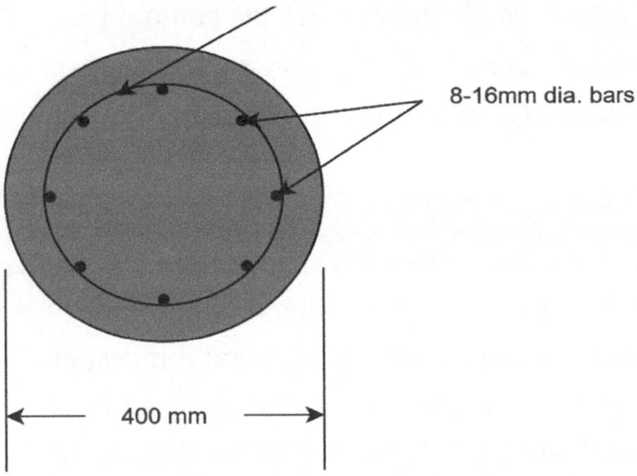

Figure 5.7: Schematic diagram of cross-section of the circular bar

SUMMARY

Reinforced Concrete (RC) columns are vertical structural elements used in building structures to transfer axial loads from the superstructure to the foundation, enhancing strength and resistance to bending moments and shear forces. The design process for an axially loaded reinforced concrete column involves determining the design loads, material properties, section selection, preliminary reinforcement, buckling consideration, strength limit state check, serviceability limit state check, and final reinforcement detailing. The design process follows the Limit State Method (LSM) as per IS 456-2000, ensuring the column meets strength and serviceability requirements. The total axial load is determined by considering all relevant loads, and the design strength of concrete and steel is determined using characteristic strengths. The cross-sectional size and shape of the column are selected based on the expected axial load, and preliminary reinforcement is estimated based on the interaction between concrete and steel.

EXERCISE

As the structural engineer working on the construction of a four-story building. Your current task is to design and analyse the columns supporting the building's loads safely and efficiently. Each group of five students will collaborate to tackle different aspects of column design and analysis based on the scenario provided. Assume data accordingly.

- Calculate the axial load from the floors above on a single column.
- Compute the effective length and classify the column type.
- Determine whether the column is short or slender based on the slenderness ratio.
- Design longitudinal and transverse reinforcement.

MULTIPLE CHOICE QUESTIONS

1. How do you define a pedestal as per IS 456-2000 based on its effective length?
   A) It should be less than 2 times its least lateral dimension
   B) It should be greater than 3 times its least lateral dimension
   C) It should be less than 3 times its least lateral dimension
   D) It should be greater than 4 times its least lateral dimension
2. How does IS 456-2000 define a column as a short column based on its slenderness ratio
   A) It should be less than equal to 12 concerning the major principal axis
   B) It should be more than 12 concerning the minor principal axis
   C) It should be less than 12 concerning both the minor principal axis as well as the major principal axis
   D) It should be greater than 12 concerning both the minor principal axis as well as the major principal axis
3. As per IS 456-2000, the effective length ratio k for a column whose one end is 'fixed' and the other is 'pinned' will be:
   A) 0.65
   B) 1.0
   C) 2.0
   D) 0.80
4. As per IS 456-2000, the minimum percentage of the cross-sectional area of longitudinal reinforcement in a column should be:
   A) 0.4 percent of gross area
   B) 6 percent of gross area
   C) 0.8 percent of gross area
   D) 4 percent of gross area
5. As per IS 456-2000, the diameter of longitudinal bars in a column should not be less than:
   A) 16 mm
   B) 12 mm
   C) 8 mm
   D) 10 mm

6. As per IS 456-2000, the minimum number of longitudinal bars in a column of a rectangular cross-section and a circular cross-section should be:
   A) 6 and 4, respectively
   B) 6 and 6, respectively
   C) 6 and 8, respectively
   D) 4 and 6, respectively
7. An axially loaded RCC column of size 350 mm x 350 mm with an unsupported length of 7m is given; the minimum eccentricity should be:
   A) 25.67 mm
   B) 20 mm
   C) 23.33 mm
   D) 28 mm
8. An RCC column of size 450 mm x 450 mm is given, having the diameters of longitudinal bars as 28 mm and 32 mm; the diameter of lateral ties should be:
   A) 6 mm
   B) 8 mm
   C) 7 mm
   D) 10 mm
9. An RCC column of size 350 mm x 350 mm is given, having the diameters of longitudinal bars as 24 mm; what should the pitch of the lateral tie be?
   A) 320 mm
   B) 350 mm
   C) 384 mm
   D) 300 mm
10. As per IS 456- 2000, the maximum spacing of lateral ties and spiral ties in a column should be:
   A) 300mm and 100 mm respectively
   B) 75 mm and 350 mm respectively
   C) 75 mm and 300 mm respectively
   D) 300 mm and 75 mm respectively

ANSWERS TO MULTIPLE CHOICE QUESTIONS

1	2	3	4	5	6	7	8
C	C	D	C	B	D	A	B
9	10						
D	D						

SHORT ANSWER TYPE QUESTIONS

1. What is the importance of the slenderness ratio in columns?
2. What are the assumptions made in the design of short columns?
3. What factors should be considered while selecting the pitch and diameter of lateral ties for columns?
4. What are braced and unbraced columns?
5. What are IS 456-2000 provisions regarding the maximum steel percentage in a column?
6. What is the limit state of compression members? Explain its importance in column design.
7. What is the effective length of a column, and how is it determined for different end conditions?
8. List the minimum steel reinforcement requirements for RCC columns as per IS 456-2000.
9. Differentiate between short and slender columns based on their behaviour under axial loads.
10. Calculate the effective length of a column with one end fixed and the other hinged, with a length of 3.5 m.
11. Determine the longitudinal reinforcement required for a circular column of diameter 500 mm diameter subjected to an axial load of 2000 kN. Assume M25 concrete and Fe 415 steel.
12. For a rectangular column with dimensions 300 mm × 500 mm, calculate the axial load-carrying capacity using M25 concrete and Fe 415 steel.

LONG ANSWER TYPE QUESTIONS

1. Design a 500 mm × 350 mm short column using M25 grade concrete and Fe 415 steel. The column is subjected to an axial load of 1200 kN under service and usual conditions of live loads. The effective length of the column is 2.8 m and is braced against side sway in both directions.
2. Design a circular short column with spiral ties using M25 grade concrete and Fe 415 steel, subjected to an axial load of 1500 kN under service load conditions.
3. A short RC column of size 350 mm × 350 mm is made of M25 grade concrete and is reinforced with a 4 no. of 20 mm diameter of Fe 500 grade. Determine the ultimate load-carrying capacity of the column, considering axial loading only.

4. A rectangular column section of size 650 mm × 400 mm of grade M20 is reinforced with 6 no. of 25 mm diameter bars of Fe 415. Determine the load-carrying capacity of the column, assuming it is an axially loaded short column.
5. Calculate the load-carrying capacity of an axially loaded short column of grade M25 concrete, circular in the section of diameter 400 mm and reinforced with 6 no. of 20 mm diameter bars of Fe 500 steel. The helical reinforcement is a 6 mm diameter of Fe 415 with a spacing of 40 mm c/c.

TUTORIAL

Consider yourself a junior structural engineer tasked with examining and assessing a column's performance and safety in a four-story residential structure. There have been reports of minor cracking in the column, which is situated near the corner of the structure. You are responsible for thoroughly examining the column, spotting any possible problems, and suggesting solutions to enhance its performance and safety.

KNOW MORE

For more information related to this topic, scan the QR code.

OR

Type this link in your browser

: https://archive.nptel.ac.in/courses/105/105/105105104/

BIBLIOGRAPHY

- Bureau of Indian Standards. (2000). IS 456:2000 - *Plain and Reinforced Concrete - Code of Practice* (4th Revision), New Delhi.
- Duggal, S. K. (2014). *Reinforced Concrete Design*, Tata McGraw Hill Education: New Delhi.
- Gambhir, M. L. (2012). *Design of Reinforced Concrete Structures*, PHI Learning Pvt. Ltd.: New Delhi

- Jain, A. K., and Jain, B. C. (2015). *Design of Reinforced Concrete Structures*, Nem Chand & Bros.: New Delhi.
- Krishna Raju, and N. Pranesh, R.N. (2018). *Reinforced Concrete Design Principles and Practice*, New Age International: Mumbai.
- Pillai, S.U., and Menon, D. (2017). *Reinforced Concrete Design*, McGraw Hill Publications: New Delhi.
- Ramamrutham, S., & Narayanan, R. (2013). *Design of Reinforced Concrete Structures*. New Delhi: Dhanpat Rai Publishing Company.
- Sinha N.C., and Roy S.K. (2007). *Fundamentals of Reinforced Concrete*, S. Chand & Co.: New Delhi.
- Varghese, P. C. (2008). *Limit State Design of Reinforced Concrete*, Prentice Hall India Learning Private Limited: Delhi.

APPENDIX A

Degree of End Restrained of Compression member	Symbol	Theoretical value of Effective length	Recommended value of effective length
Effectively held in position and restrained against rotation in both ends	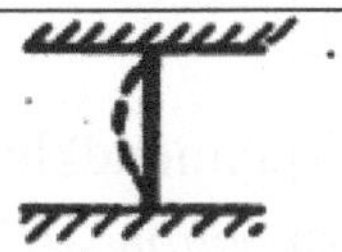	0.5l	0.65l
Effectively held in position at both ends, restrained against rotation at one end	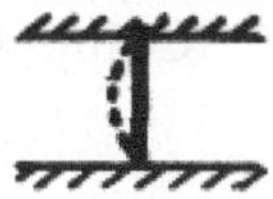	0.7l	0.8l
Effectively held in position at both ends, but not restrained against rotation.	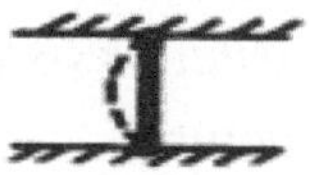	1.00l	1.00l
Effectively held in position and restrained against rotation at one end and at the other restrained against rotation but not held in position.		1.00l	1.20l
Effectively held in position and restrained against rotation at one end and at the other partially restrained against rotation but not held in position.	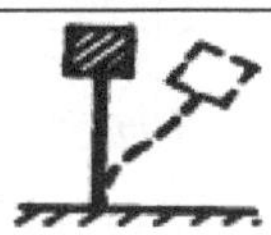	-	1.50l
Effectively held in position at one end but not restrained against rotation, and at the other end restrained against rotation but not held in position.	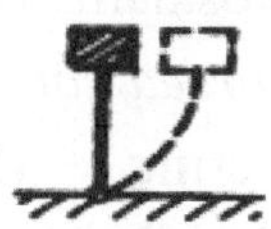	2.00l	2.00l
Effectively held in position and restrained against rotation at one end but not held in position nor restrained against rotation lit the other end.	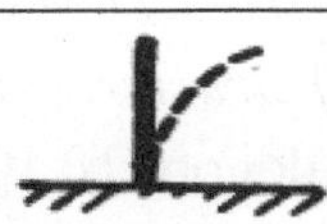	2.00l	2.00l

B REFERENCES FOR FURTHER LEARNING

- Andrade, C., Alonso, C., & Molina, F. J. (1993). *Cover cracking as a function of bar corrosion: Part I-Experimental test.* Materials and Structures, 26(8), 453–464. https://doi.org/10.1007/BF02472805

- Cha, Y.-J., Choi, W., Suh, G., Mahmoudkhani, S., & Büyüköztürk, O. (2018). *Autonomous structural visual inspection using region-based deep learning for detecting multiple damage types.* Computer-Aided Civil and Infrastructure Engineering, 33(9), 731–747. https://doi.org/10.1111/mice.12334

- Christopoulos, C., Tremblay, R., Kim, H.-J., & Lacerte, M. (2008). *Self-centring energy dissipative bracing system for the seismic resistance of structures: Development and validation.* Journal of Structural Engineering, 134(1), 96–107. https://doi.org/10.1061/(ASCE)0733-9445(2008)134:1(96)

- Coronelli, D., & Gambarova, P. (2004). *Structural assessment of corroded reinforced concrete beams: Modeling guidelines.* Journal of Structural Engineering, 130(8), 1214–1224. https://doi.org/10.1061/(ASCE)0733-9445(2004)130:8(1214)

- Coronelli, D., & Gambarova, P. (2004). *Structural assessment of corroded reinforced concrete beams: Modeling guidelines.* Journal of Structural Engineering, 130(8), 1214–1224. https://doi.org/10.1061/(ASCE)0733-9445(2004)130:8(1214)

- Gardoni, P., Der Kiureghian, A., & Mosalam, K. M. (2002). *Probabilistic capacity models and fragility estimates for reinforced concrete columns based on experimental observations.* Journal of Engineering Mechanics, 128(10), 1024–1038. https://doi.org/10.1061/(ASCE)0733-9399(2002)128:10(1024)

- Han, L.-H., Li, W., & Bjorhovde, R. (2014). *Developments and advanced applications of concrete-filled steel tubular (CFST) structures: Members.* Journal of Constructional Steel Research, 100, 211–228. https://doi.org/10.1016/j.jcsr.2014.04.016

- Han, L.-H., Yao, G.-H., & Zhao, X.-L. (2005). *Tests and calculations for hollow structural steel (HSS) stub columns filled with self-consolidating concrete (SCC).*

Journal of Constructional Steel Research, 61(9), 1241–1269. https://doi.org/10.1016/j.jcsr.2005.01.004

- Kalkan, E., & Kunnath, S. K. (2006). *Effects of fling step and forward directivity on seismic response of buildings.* Earthquake Spectra, 22(2), 367–390. https://doi.org/10.1193/1.2192560

- Mirmiran, A., & Shahawy, M. (1997). *Behavior of concrete columns confined by fibre composites.* Journal of Structural Engineering, 123(5), 583–590. https://doi.org/10.1061/(ASCE)0733-9445(1997)123:5(583)

- Park, Y.-J., Ang, A. H.-S., & Wen, Y. K. (1985). *Seismic damage analysis of reinforced concrete buildings.* Journal of Structural Engineering, 111(4), 740–757. https://doi.org/10.1061/(ASCE)0733-9445(1985)111:4(740)

- Reddy, B. V. V., & Jagadish, K. S. (2003). *Embodied energy of common and alternative building materials and technologies.* Energy and Buildings, 35(2), 129–137. https://doi.org/10.1016/S0378-7788(01)00141-4

- Sabelli, R., Mahin, S., & Chang, C. (2003). *Seismic demands on steel-braced frame buildings with buckling-restrained braces.* Engineering Structures, 25(5), 655–666. https://doi.org/10.1016/S0141-0296(02)00175-X

- Sakino, K., Nakahara, H., Morino, S., & Nishiyama, I. (2004). *Behavior of centrally loaded concrete-filled steel-tube short columns.* Journal of Structural Engineering, 130(2), 180–188. https://doi.org/10.1061/(ASCE)0733-9445(2004)130:2(180)

- Schafer, B. W. (2008). *Review: The direct strength method of cold-formed steel member design.* Journal of Constructional Steel Research, 64(7–8), 766–778. https://doi.org/10.1016/j.jcsr.2008.01.022

- Schafer, B. W., & Peköz, T. (1998). *Computational modelling of cold-formed steel: Characterizing geometric imperfections and residual stresses.* Journal of Constructional Steel Research, 47(3), 193–210. https://doi.org/10.1016/S0143-974X(98)00007-8

- Scott, B. D., Park, R., & Priestley, M. J. N. (1982). *Stress-strain behaviour of concrete confined by overlapping hoops at low and high strain rates.* Journal of the American Concrete Institute, 79(1), 13–27.

- Shi, X., Xie, N., Fortune, K., & Gong, J. (2012). *Durability of steel reinforced concrete in chloride environments: An overview.* Construction and Building Materials, 30, 125–138. https://doi.org/10.1016/j.conbuildmat.2011.12.038
- Singh, B., Ishwarya, G., Gupta, M., & Bhattacharyya, S. K. (2015). *Geopolymer concrete: A review of some recent developments.* Construction and Building Materials, 85, 78–90. https://doi.org/10.1016/j.conbuildmat.2015.03.036
- Song, G., Ma, N., & Li, H.-N. (2006). *Applications of shape memory alloys in civil structures.* Engineering Structures, 28(9), 1266–1274. https://doi.org/10.1016/j.engstruct.2005.12.010
- Tao, Z., Wang, Z.-B., & Yu, Q. (2013). *Finite element modelling of concrete-filled steel stub columns under axial compression.* Journal of Constructional Steel Research, 89, 121–131. https://doi.org/10.1016/j.jcsr.2013.07.001
- Teng, J. G., Yu, T., & Fernando, D. (2012). *Strengthening of steel structures with fiber-reinforced polymer composites.* Journal of Constructional Steel Research, 78, 131–143. https://doi.org/10.1016/j.jcsr.2012.06.011
- Vecchio, F. J., & Collins, M. P. (1986). *Modified compression-field theory for reinforced concrete elements subjected to shear.* Journal of the American Concrete Institute, 83(2), 219–231.
- Walling, S. A., & Provis, J. L. (2016). *Magnesia-based cement: A journey of 150 years, and cement for the future?* Chemical Reviews, 116(7), 4170–4204. https://doi.org/10.1021/acs.chemrev.5b00463
- Xiao, J., Qiang, C., Nanni, A., & Zhang, K. (2017). *Use of sea sand and seawater in concrete construction: Current status and future opportunities.* Construction and Building Materials, 155, 1101–1111. https://doi.org/10.1016/j.conbuildmat.2017.08.130
- Yoo, D.-Y., & Banthia, N. (2016). *Mechanical properties of ultra-high-performance fiber-reinforced concrete: A review.* Cement and Concrete Composites, 73, 267–280. https://doi.org/10.1016/j.cemconcomp.2016.08.001

- Zhao, X.-L., & Zhang, L. (2007). *State-of-the-art review on FRP-strengthened steel structures.* Engineering Structures, 29(8), 1808–1823. https://doi.org/10.1016/j.engstruct.2006.10.006
- Zollo, R. F. (1997). *Fiber-reinforced concrete: An overview after 30 years of development.* Cement and Concrete Composites, 19(2), 107–122. https://doi.org/10.1016/s0958-9465(96)00046-7

C CO AND PO ATTAINABLE TABLE

Course outcomes (COs) for this course can be mapped with the programme outcomes (POs) after the completion of the course, and a correlation can be made for the attainment of POs to analyse the gap. After proper analysis of the gap in attaining POs, necessary measures can be taken to overcome the gaps.

Table for CO and PO attainment

Course Outcomes	Expected Mapping with Programme Outcomes (1- Weak correlation; 2- Medium correlation; 3- Strong correlation)						
	PO-1	PO-2	PO-3	PO-4	PO-5	PO-6	PO-7
CO-1							
CO-2							
CO-3							
CO-4							
CO-5							

The data filled in the above table can be used for gap analysis.

D INDEX